Palgrave Studies in Victims and Victimology

In recent decades, a growing emphasis on meeting the needs and rights of victims of crime in criminal justice policy and practice has fuelled the development of research, theory, policy and practice outcomes stretching across the globe. This growth of interest in the victim of crime has seen victimology move from being a distinct subset of criminology in academia to a specialist area of study and research in its own right. *Palgrave Studies in Victims and Victimology* showcases the work of contemporary scholars of victimological research and publishes some of the highest-quality research in the field. The series reflects the range and depth of research and scholarship in this burgeoning area, combining contributions from both established scholars who have helped to shape the field and more recent entrants. It also reflects both the global nature of many of the issues surrounding justice for victims of crime and social harm and the international span of scholarship researching and writing about them.

Sophie Mortimer · Andy Phippen ·
Emma Bond

Ten Years of the Revenge Porn Helpline

Understanding the Evolution of Intimate Image Abuse: Policy, Practice and Victim Support

palgrave
macmillan

Sophie Mortimer
South-West Grid for Learning
Exeter, UK

Andy Phippen
Bournemouth University
Poole, UK

Emma Bond
University of Suffolk
Ipswich, Suffolk, UK

ISSN 2947-9355 ISSN 2947-9363 (electronic)
Palgrave Studies in Victims and Victimology
ISBN 978-3-032-00613-4 ISBN 978-3-032-00614-1 (eBook)
https://doi.org/10.1007/978-3-032-00614-1

This Palgrave Macmillan imprint is published by the registered company Springer Nature Switzerland AG
The registered company address is: Gewerbestrasse 11, 6330 Cham, Switzerland

Competing Interests The authors have no competing interests to declare that are relevant to the content of this manuscript.

Contents

List of Tables

1

Introduction

Abstract This introductory chapter lays the foundation for a comprehensive examination of Non-Consensual Intimate Image (NCII) abuse, commonly mischaracterized as "revenge pornography". It contextualizes the phenomenon within broader socio-legal, technological, and gendered frameworks, and critiques prevailing terminology that obscures the complexity and harm of image-based sexual abuse. The chapter outlines the psychological impacts on victims, inadequacies in legal responses, gendered dimensions of abuse, and the role of digital platforms in facilitating or mitigating harm. Central to the discussion is the UK's Revenge Porn Helpline (RPH), a decade-long case study that provides empirical insights into the scale, modalities, and evolving nature of NCII. Through analysis of over 22,000 cases, AI-assisted thematic and sentiment analyses, stakeholder interviews, and ethnographic reflection, the chapter argues for a systemic, ecosystem-based approach to understanding and addressing NCII. The work foregrounds survivor agency and cross-sector collaboration as vital to sustainable and effective intervention. Ultimately, this book calls for a paradigm shift—from fragmented legal remedies and reactive platform moderation to integrated, trauma-informed, and preventative strategies.

S. Mortimer et al., *Ten Years of the Revenge Porn Helpline*, Palgrave Studies in Victims and Victimology, https://doi.org/10.1007/978-3-032-00614-1_1

Keywords Non-Consensual Intimate Images (NCII) · Image · Based sexual abuse · Digital gender · Based violence · Platform accountability · Revenge Porn Helpline

Revenge pornography, also known as Non-Consensual Intimate Images (NCII) or Intimate Image Abuse (IIA), involves the distribution of sexually explicit images or videos without the subject's consent, often by ex-partners as a form of retaliation. The advent of smartphones and social media platforms has significantly contributed to the proliferation of this form of abuse. This literature review examines scholarly discussions surrounding the psychological impact on victims, legal responses, gender dynamics, and the responsibility of digital platforms.

According to Henry and Powell (2015), revenge pornography is a type of image-based sexual abuse that includes not only the distribution of intimate images but also the threat of such distribution, which can have similarly devastating effects. Phippen and Brennan (2020) argue that the phrase is misleading because it suggests a motive of personal revenge, which does not account for the full range of reasons why non-consensual intimate images might be shared. Acts of this nature can be driven by a desire for control, humiliation, or profit, not just retaliation. They also note that the use of the term "revenge" can lead to victim-blaming. It implies that the victim did something to provoke the perpetrator, which shifts the focus away from the abuser's actions and undermines support for the person harmed. Furthermore, the term "pornography" inaccurately implies consent and mutual participation. This is particularly problematic because the images or videos in question are distributed without consent, and the label minimizes the seriousness of the violation.

McGlynn et al. (2017) emphasize the broader spectrum of "image-based sexual abuse", arguing that the term "revenge porn" is misleading as it suggests motivation rooted in revenge and excludes other contexts, such as profit or entertainment.

Victims of revenge pornography often experience profound psychological harm, including anxiety, depression, PTSD, and social withdrawal (Bates, 2017). Walker and Sleath (2017) found that victims frequently report feeling powerless and violated, with long-lasting effects on their self-esteem and interpersonal relationships. The public and often viral nature of the abuse exacerbates the trauma, making recovery more challenging (Citron & Franks, 2014).

Legal responses to revenge pornography vary widely across jurisdictions. In the USA, many states have enacted specific laws criminalizing non-consensual pornography (Citron & Franks, 2014). However, critics argue that these laws are inconsistently enforced and often fail to capture the nuances of digital abuse. In the UK, the Criminal Justice and Courts Act 2015 made it a criminal offence to disclose private sexual photographs without consent, intending to cause distress. Yet, McGlynn et al. (2017) argue that requiring proof of intent to distress limits the law's effectiveness.

Revenge pornography is a gendered phenomenon. Studies show that women are disproportionately targeted, often by male partners seeking to shame or control them (Powell & Henry, 2017). The abuse intersects with misogynistic online cultures that commodify women's bodies and perpetuate gender-based violence. Bates (2017) highlights that female victims often face victim-blaming attitudes, which compound the harm and deter reporting. However, as we will explore in subsequent chapters, it is a crime that impacts upon male victims too, with sextortion being the dominant impact here.

Digital platforms such as Facebook, Reddit, and Pornhub have faced criticism for enabling the dissemination of non-consensual images. Gillespie (2018) points out the tension between platform neutrality and content moderation, arguing that tech companies have been slow to implement effective safeguards. Recent legislative efforts, such as the EARN IT Act in the USA, aim to hold platforms more accountable, though they raise concerns about privacy and censorship (Franks, 2020).

Against this backdrop, the Revenge Porn Helpline,[1] launched in 2015 by SWGfL[2] as part of the UK Safer Internet Centre,[3] represents a pioneering institutional response to NCII. It was the UK's first dedicated service for adults affected by this form of abuse and has, over its first

---

[1] https://revengepornhelpline.org.uk/. Accessed May 2025.

[2] https://www.swgfl.org.uk/. Accessed May 2025.

[3] https://saferinternet.org.uk/. Accessed May 2025.

ten years, evolved from a reactive support line into a multi-functional actor within what we now conceptualize as the *online safety ecosystem* (Phippen & Bond, 2024). The Helpline supports victims, liaises with platforms and law enforcement, contributes to legal reform, and collects one of the most comprehensive empirical datasets available on NCII incidents in the UK. This book, then, is both a chronicle and a critique: it is a record of the RP Helpline's development, achievements, and challenges, and a scholarly intervention into the broader debates surrounding digital abuse, legal reform, platform accountability and stakeholder responsibilities. It is also a reflection on what can be achieved if stakeholders work in partnership to their strength and with a common purpose.

At its core, this book poses several interrelated questions: How has NCII evolved in terms of its modalities, perpetrators, and impacts? What role have legal reforms played in redressing harm and where have they fallen short? How do platforms operationalize their responsibilities in the wake of mounting public and legislative pressure? And most critically, how do victims navigate the multifaceted landscape of justice-seeking in a system where laws exist, but recourse remains elusive?

To answer these questions, this book draws upon a mixed-methods research design. The empirical foundation includes:

- A decade of anonymized case records from the Helpline over 2024 (approximately 22,000 cases) that provide insights into the nature of NCII abuse impact on victims today
- Qualitative interviews with helpline practitioners and other stakeholders around the helpline,
- Statistics drawn from secondary sources, primarily annual reports from the Revenge Porn Helpline but also other public data sources,
- Freedom of Information data collected from UK police forces and the Crown Prosecution Service (CPS), revealing the rates-and obstacles-of arrests, prosecutions, and convictions,
- And a review of policy, case law, academic literature, and media coverage, situating the Helpline's work within both national and international contexts.

Due to the size of the qualitative data sets used to explore case descriptions, we have utilized AI tools to perform sentiment and thematic analysis, which allows us to uncover deeper insights and streamline the review of complex and sizable textual information. By applying natural language processing techniques, we were able to process thousands of case reports efficiently, extracting key themes and emotional trends that would have been difficult to detect manually. We conducted thematic analysis to identify recurring topics, such as patterns in victim statements, the nature of abuse, law enforcement response, support from other stakeholders and impact.

In parallel, we implemented sentiment analysis to gauge the tone and emotional undercurrents within the case narratives. This allowed us to recognize areas of concern and sensitivity and better understand victim perspectives. The combination of thematic and sentiment insights provided a more holistic view of the data, allowing for a deeper understanding of the data set and more nuanced reporting.

Given the black box nature of the AI analysis, this was verified with helpline practitioners (one of whom is a co-author on this book), to ensure that findings from the analysis were consistent with their lived experience.

Furthermore, there is also a significant ethnography element to this exploration. We have all been working for, and with, the Revenge Porn Helpline over the majority of its existence, in both participation and management (Sophie), research (Emma and Andy) and strategic as a trustee (Andy).

As such we are uniquely positioned to reflect upon the development of the helpline, the ecosystem around it, and to consider how the helpline has, somewhat unusually for an actor in the online harms ecosystem, been extremely evidence led. We position the Helpline as a unique actor-one that not only responds to harm but also produces knowledge about systemic gaps and has demonstrated success in closing those gaps through the implementation of changes to process and legislation. Through daily contact with victims, stakeholders, and engagement with platforms and takedown systems, the Helpline is uniquely placed to observe where laws fail to protect, where institutions resist adaptation, and where harm becomes facilitated through digital infrastructures. Given this book is a collaboration between the Revenge Porn Helpline manager and two academics who have collaborated with the helpline over its entire life, the presentation in this book will be a mix of academic discourse and practice reflections, drawing heavily on empirical data. As such, some chapters will look more broadly at the body of knowledge and academic literature, whereas others will almost entirely look at the experiences and data from the helpline.

Conceptually, this book interrogates how NCII has been framed and responded to in policy and practice-often shaped by gendered assumptions, technological determinism, and a misplaced reliance on criminal law as a singular solution. The notion of an "online safety ecosystem", as articulated by Phippen and Bond (2024), provides a central analytical lens towards the end of the book as a means to address the complexities of this topic. This ecosystem approach resists the reductive tendency to isolate law, tech, criminal justice and victim services. Instead, it recognizes that meaningful change requires interconnected reforms across platform design, enforcement practices, education systems, cultural narratives, and long-term victim support.

The Scale of the Issue

The rapid expansion of digital communication and social media has significantly heightened the risks associated with Non-Consensual Intimate Image (NCII) abuse. These platforms have made it easier than ever to create, disseminate, and exploit intimate content without consent. Although the UK has been at the forefront of criminalizing NCII-introducing legislation a decade ago, the problem continues to escalate globally. According to the 2024 Revenge Porn Helpline (RPH) Report (Revenge Porn Helpline, 2024), over 22,000 cases were recorded in a single year, marking a tenfold increase since 2019 (Revenge Porn Helpline, 2020). This alarming surge points to an urgent need for more comprehensive policies, enhanced victim support systems, and stronger technological interventions to combat the widespread distribution of NCII content.

In the UK, NCII abuse is rising at a pace, mirroring broader patterns of tech-facilitated gender-based violence (Dlamini, 2021). This increase reflects not only a greater number of incidents but also improvements in detection mechanisms and growing public awareness. Nonetheless, underreporting remains a major challenge, concealing the full extent of the issue. This is something we explore in detail throughout this book.

The chapters in this book present empirical findings that underline the severe psychological and social harm inflicted by NCII. Victims frequently encounter major obstacles when seeking justice—including inconsistent legal protections, delayed or inadequate responses from platforms, unsatisfactory law enforcement action, and fear of retaliation.

As discussed, the steady rise in cases handled by the Revenge Porn Helpline starkly illustrates NCII's growing footprint in the UK. Since its launch, the Helpline has seen cases increase from 521 in 2015 to over 22,000 in 2024, representing a more than 40-fold escalation. While this reflects improved service accessibility and a greater willingness among victims to seek help, it also signals a deeper entrenchment of NCII as a persistent and pervasive form of digital abuse.

If current trends continue, projections suggest that annual caseloads may surpass 46,000 by 2028. This indicates not just a rising trend but a full-blown crisis requiring urgent and systemic intervention. The actual prevalence of NCII is likely much higher than reported figures imply, as many victims remain silent due to stigma, distrust of authorities, and limited faith in platform accountability-factors thoroughly examined in this book. Furthermore, very few reported cases result in conviction, highlighting significant gaps in justice delivery.

Extensive research into online harms reveals a stark disparity between reported incidents and the actual number of victims (Dworkin et al., 2021). It is estimated that for every reported case, many others go unreported due to fear, lack of awareness, or perceived ineffectiveness of formal recourse.

While the UK has made notable progress in developing laws and policies to address NCII-often leading international efforts-significant gaps remain in enforcement, victim care, and cross-border collaboration.

To assess the global impact of NCII, we can extrapolate data using broader Violence Against Women and Girls (VAWG) statistics, aligning these with findings from the Helpline. By quantifying both the number of individuals affected and the scale of non-consensual image circulation, we gain a clearer understanding of the scope of the issue.

Our analysis begins with the UK, focusing on the adult female population, as women are disproportionately targeted in NCII cases (Revenge Porn Helpline, 2023). By applying known prevalence rates from both governmental and NGO sources, we can estimate the actual volume of NCII incidents, the scale of content creation and dissemination, and the deficiencies within current reporting structures.

Based on UK Government and non-governmental sources:

- Total adult female population (UK): 26,064,118 (Office for National Statistics, 2023).
- Annual prevalence of gender-based violence (GBV) among women: 8.3% (National Police Chief's Council, 2023).
- Percentage of GBV cases involving NCII: 17% (Refuge, 2022).

The report highlights the widespread nature of online harassment, with NCII forming a significant component of technology-facilitated gender-based violence.

We estimate that annual NCII victims, using this data, would be 369,272. This figure is derived by applying the NPCC estimate that 8.3% of adult women experience gender-based violence (GBV) annually to the total UK adult female population of 26,064,118 (ibid.).

Based on data from the 2023 Revenge Porn Helpline (RPH) Annual Report (Revenge Porn Helpline, 2023), it is estimated that each NCII case involving an adult female victim contains an average of 8.6 non-consensually shared images. This figure, drawn from direct casework, highlights the extent of image proliferation per individual and underscores that the impact of NCII often extends well beyond a single incident. While 8.6 is the average, the Helpline has documented cases where victims had tens of thousands of images distributed without their consent. The report also reveals that these images are frequently shared across multiple platforms, with repeated uploads significantly amplifying the harm caused.

Using this average, we estimate that approximately 3.18 million NCII images are generated and distributed annually in the UK. This figure is derived by multiplying the estimated number of annual victims (369,272) by the average number of images per case (8.6), as reported in the 2023 RPH Annual Report. This calculation demonstrates the vast and ongoing scale of NCII content circulating each year, reinforcing the urgency of effective intervention.

The same modelling indicates that NCII impacts approximately 1.42% of all adult women in the UK each year. This estimate is based on dividing the number of projected victims (369,272) by the total adult female population (26,064,118), as reported by the Office for National Statistics (ONS, 2023). This prevalence rate positions NCII alongside Child Sexual Abuse Material (CSAM) in terms of scope and seriousness.

To validate this comparison, we turn to the 2023 National Centre for Missing and Exploited Children CyberTipline Report (National Center for Missing & Exploited Children, 2023). An analysis of CSAM reports relative to child population sizes in Five Eyes nations reveals prevalence rates ranging from 1.24% in the UK to 1.54% in Canada, with a Five Eyes average of 1.47%. These figures closely align with the 1.42% prevalence rate for NCII among adult women in the UK, reinforcing the conclusion that NCII constitutes a digital harm of comparable scale and urgency to CSAM.

Despite the scope suggested by these estimates, NCII remains drastically underreported. In 2023, the Revenge Porn Helpline assisted approximately 9,000 adult female victims through a combination of direct casework and chatbot support. When compared to the projected 369,272 victims, this indicates that for every woman who receives assistance, around 53 others do not, illustrating the stark gap between reported and actual cases and highlighting the so-called iceberg effect, where most incidents remain hidden.

Further data obtained via a Freedom of Information (FOI) request, discussed in more detail in Chapter 4, reveals that in 2024, 37 UK police forces received 6459 NCII-related complaints. These led to 1037 arrests and just 264 outcomes involving cautions or charges, amounting to only 4% of cases resulting in criminal action. Additionally, in 2180 cases, victims withdrew their support for the investigation, suggesting systemic barriers to justice and the emotional toll of pursuing legal action.

To understand NCII at a broader level, the Five Eyes alliance—comprising the UK, USA, Canada, Australia, and New Zealand—offers a useful framework. By applying the UK's estimated prevalence rate (1.42% of adult women) to the adult female populations of these countries, we can approximate the potential scale of NCII across allied nations with comparable digital ecosystems and legal structures. This approach enables cross-national comparisons, highlights potential reporting and enforcement gaps, and emphasizes the need for coordinated international action to address NCII as a growing cybercrime threat.

Country	Adult Female Population	Estimated Annual NCII Victims	Estimated Annual NCII Images
United Kingdom	26.06 million	369,272	3.18 million
United States	126.1 million	1.79 million	15.4 million
Canada	19.4 million	275,000	2.37 million
Australia	13.2 million	187,000	1.62 million
New Zealand	4.2 million	59,000	515,000
Total	189 million	2.67 million	22.99 million

These figures suggest that the Five Eyes nations alone generate nearly 23 million NCII images annually, a number comparable to global CSAM reporting.

Using prevalence data from the Five Eyes nations, particularly the UK, it is possible to estimate the global scale of Non-Consensual Intimate Image (NCII) abuse. The UK's estimated annual prevalence rate—1.42% of adult women—can be applied to the global adult female population to approximate both the number of affected individuals and the volume of NCII content generated each year.

Key calculations:

- Estimated global adult female population: ~3.5 billion (United Nations, 2023)
- Estimated NCII victims annually (1.42%): ~49.7 million
- Average NCII images per victim: 8.6
- Estimated NCII images generated annually: ~428 million

This projection indicates a substantial volume of NCII material being created and shared worldwide each year. For comparison, the National Center for Missing and Exploited Children (NCMEC) reported 35.9 million global CSAM reports in 2023 via its CyberTipline. Using the above estimates, a global reporting infrastructure for NCII could expect to receive approximately 63.4 million reports per year, suggesting that NCII cases may exceed CSAM reports by around 76% in scale.

This comparison highlights the high volume of NCII cases relative to other forms of online image-based abuse. Unlike CSAM, which benefits from structured global reporting mechanisms and mandatory reporting requirements in many countries, NCII reporting systems remain decentralized. As a result, case management, victim access to support, and law enforcement responses vary significantly between jurisdictions.

The implications of this comparison are substantial. A coordinated global NCII reporting and response mechanism, like the CSAM model, would enable authorities to better track, prevent, and respond to NCII incidents. Furthermore, industry collaboration through hash-sharing and automated detection could significantly reduce the circulation of non-consensual imagery, improving victim protection and legal enforcement. This comparison highlights the necessity of treating NCII as a major cyber-enabled crime, requiring the same level of urgency and international cooperation as CSAM. This is something we will return to towards the end of the book.

Ten Years of the Revenge Porn Helpline

This volume documents and critically analyses ten years of the UK's *Revenge Porn Helpline* (RPH), contextualizing its emergence, evolution, and impact within broader socio-legal, technological, and policy frameworks. Founded in 2015 in response to rising awareness of non-consensual image sharing and the limitations of existing legal remedies, the Helpline has become an internationally recognized model of victim-centred intervention and advocacy. Through empirical data, case studies, legal analysis, and practitioner insights, this book interrogates the shifting contours of intimate image abuse (IIA) and situates the RPH's work within a broader ecosystem of state, platform, and civil society responses. The chapters provide both retrospective reflection and forward-looking critique, offering a comprehensive understanding of the challenges and opportunities in addressing IIA as a complex, multifaceted social harm.

Chapter 2 charts the institutional development of the Revenge Porn Helpline over its first decade, beginning with its formation within the South West Grid for Learning and its early interactions with law enforcement, victims, and digital platforms. This chapter offers a narrative and empirical review of the service's operational growth, highlighting the increasing complexity of cases—ranging from traditional "revenge porn" to sextortion, synthetic media, and anonymous mass-sharing. It also explores the impact of major events such as the COVID-19 pandemic, which exacerbated digital harms, and assesses landmark developments like the launch of *StopNCII.org* and the integration of AI tools in victim triage and content moderation.

Chapter 3 examines the legislative journey of IIA in the UK. It provides a doctrinal analysis of the evolution from fragmented pre-digital statutes—such as the Malicious Communications Act 1988 and the Protection from Harassment Act 1997—to more targeted criminal offences introduced in the Criminal Justice and Courts Act 2015, the Domestic Abuse Act 2021, and the Online Safety Act 2023. Particular attention is given to the gaps exposed by the Helpline's casework, such as the exclusion of deepfakes and threats to share, the narrow definition of "intimate", and the original requirement for "intent to cause distress". The chapter draws on policy consultation processes, including the Law Commission's 2021 review, to evaluate the effectiveness and limitations of the evolving legal landscape.

Chapter 4 centres victim experiences, using qualitative data drawn from helpline cases, court judgments, and survivor narratives to interrogate the real-world application of legal remedies. It critically engages with concepts of justice, re-traumatization, and institutional failure, showing how many victims remain underserved by criminal justice pathways. High-profile cases are juxtaposed with anonymized accounts to illustrate disparities in access, perception, and outcome. This chapter argues for a reorientation of legal and procedural frameworks around trauma-informed, survivor-centred principles, beyond punitive justice alone.

Chapter 5 interrogates the diversity of victim experiences, challenging the persistent reliance on stereotypical victim-perpetrator binaries. Drawing on intersectional theory, the chapter highlights how gender, race, age, sexual orientation, and cultural background shape the nature, experience, and consequences of IIA. Empirical data from the Helpline is used to show disparities in case typologies-such as the gendered nature of sextortion and the cultural framing of honour and shame. The chapter advocates for a more nuanced and inclusive understanding of harm, one that resists universalizing assumptions and better informs legal and policy responses.

Chapter 6 applies an ecological systems framework to understand IIA as a product of multiple, interacting systems from individual perpetration to structural inequalities. Using Bronfenbrenner's theory, the chapter maps the interdependencies between personal relationships, institutional actors (e.g. schools, police, tech platforms), and wider cultural norms. It argues that effective intervention must address all layers of this ecosystem simultaneously, recognizing that IIA is not an isolated act but embedded within broader systems of gendered power, digital culture, and regulatory failure.

Chapter 7 turns to technological responses to IIA, offering a critical examination of the use of digital fingerprinting, perceptual hashing, and chatbot-assisted triage in preventing and mitigating harm. The chapter documents the development and uptake of *StopNCII.org*, reflecting on its novel decentralized, privacy-preserving architecture. It also evaluates the limits of technological interventions, cautioning against over-reliance on automated tools in the absence of strong legal mandates, cultural change, and human-centred design. The discussion engages with current debates on ethical AI, content moderation, and platform accountability.

Chapter 8 situates the work of the RPH within the global landscape, exploring opportunities for cross-jurisdictional collaboration, standard-setting, and systemic reform. It outlines the potential for *StopNCII.org* to become a global standard for pre-emptive takedown, supported by multi-stakeholder governance and enhanced legal mandates. The chapter advocates for a coordinated, global ecosystem of victim support and concludes with recommendations for sustainable funding, capacity-building, and the establishment of a global clearinghouse akin to NCMEC for non-consensual intimate imagery.

In bringing together these chapters, this book offers a practitioner-informed, and empirically grounded contribution to the literature on image-based abuse. It affirms the centrality of survivor agency and front-line expertise in shaping meaningful responses to digital sexual harm and calls for a paradigm shift-from fragmented reaction to systemic prevention.

References

Bates, S. (2017). Revenge pornography and mental health: A qualitative analysis of the mental health effects of revenge pornography. *Feminist Criminology, 12*(1), 22–42.

Citron, D. K., & Franks, M. A. (2014). Criminalizing revenge porn. *Wake Forest Law Review, 49*, 345–391.

Dlamini, N. J. (2021). Gender-based violence, twin pandemic to COVID-19. *Critical Sociology, 47*(4–5), 583–590.

Dworkin, E. R., Krahé, B., & Zinzow, H. (2021). The global prevalence of sexual assault: A systematic review of international research since 2010. *Psychology of Violence, 11*(5), 497.

Franks, M. A. (2020). *The lawless internet? Myths and realities*. Huffington Post Blog. https://www.huffpost.com/entry/section-230-the-lawless-internet_b_4455090

Gillespie, T. (2018). *Custodians of the Internet: Platforms, content moderation, and the hidden decisions that shape social media*. Yale University Press.

Henry, N., & Powell, A. (2015). Embodied harms: Gender, shame, and technology-facilitated sexual violence. *Violence Against Women, 21*(6), 758–779.

McGlynn, C., Rackley, E., & Houghton, R. (2017). Beyond 'revenge porn': The continuum of image-based sexual abuse. *Feminist Legal Studies, 25*(1), 25–46.

National Center for Missing and Exploited Children. (2023). *CyberTipline Reports*. https://www.missingkids.org/content/dam/missingkids/pdfs/2023-CyberTipline-Report.pdf. Accessed May 2025.

National Police Chief's Council. (2023). *Call to Action as Violence Against Women and Girls Epidemic Deepens.* https://news.npcc.police.uk/releases/call-to-action-as-violence-against-women-and-girls-epidemic-deepens-1. Accessed May 2025.

Office for National Statistics. (2023). *Population estimates for England and Wales: mid-2023.* https://www.ons.gov.uk/peoplepopulationandcommunity/populationandmigration/populationestimates/bulletins/populationestimatesforenglandandwales/mid2023/pdf. Accessed May 2025.

Phippen, A., & Bond, E. (2024). Why do legislators keep failing victims in online harms? *International Review of Law, Computers & Technology, 38*(2), 195–214.

Phippen, A., & Brennan, M. (2020). *Sexting and revenge pornography: Legislative and social dimensions of a modern digital phenomenon.* Routledge.

Powell, A., & Henry, N. (2017). *Sexual violence in a digital age.* Palgrave Macmillan.

Refuge. (2022). *Unsocial Spaces: Online Harassment and NCII Abuse.* https://refuge.org.uk/wp-content/uploads/2022/06/Unsocial-Spaces.pdf. Accessed May 2025.

Revenge Porn Helpline. (2020). *Intimate Image Abuse: An Evolving Landscape.* https://revengepornhelpline.org.uk/assets/documents/intimate-image-abuse-an-evolving-landscape.pdf. Accessed May 2025.

Revenge Porn Helpline. (2023). *Annual Report 2023.* https://revengepornhelpline.org.uk/assets/documents/revenge-porn-helpline-report-2023.pdf. Accessed May 2025.

Revenge Porn Helpline. (2024). *Annual Report 2024.* https://swgfl.org.uk/assets/documents/revenge-porn-helpline-2024-annual-report.pdf. Accessed May 2025.

United Nations. (2023). *World Population Data.* https://www.un.org/en/global-issues/population. Accessed May 2025.

Walker, K., & Sleath, E. (2017). A systematic review of the psychological consequences of revenge pornography. *Aggression and Violent Behavior, 36*, 219–226.

2

The Revenge Porn Helpline Then and Now: A Review of Ten Years of Operation

Abstract This chapter chronicles the ten-year evolution of the UK's Revenge Porn Helpline (RPH), contextualizing its emergence, development, and growing influence within the broader online safety ecosystem. From its founding in 2015 as a pilot service responding to intimate image abuse, the chapter details how the Helpline has become a globally recognized actor in victim support, advocacy, and technological innovation—most notably through its co-development of *StopNCII.org*. Drawing on practitioner experiences, policy engagement, and historical case data, the chapter highlights key milestones and persistent challenges in law enforcement collaboration, victim-blaming narratives, and systemic gaps in justice delivery. It assesses the Helpline's responses to critical turning points, including the COVID-19 pandemic, legislative reforms, and the rise of synthetic and AI-generated imagery. It also evaluates the enduring limitations of criminal justice systems and underscores the importance of proactive, victim-centric strategies that integrate legal, technological, and cultural change. The chapter serves as both a retrospective and a strategic overview, offering critical insights into the evolution of digital abuse and the institutional responses required to meaningfully combat intimate image abuse at scale.

S. Mortimer et al., *Ten Years of the Revenge Porn Helpline*, Palgrave Studies in Victims and Victimology, https://doi.org/10.1007/978-3-032-00614-1_2

Keywords Revenge Porn Helpline · Intimate image abuse · StopNCII.org · Victim support services · Online safety ecosystem

This chapter traces the Helpline's journey over ten years: from its origins within the broader framework of online safety, through early challenges in securing justice and support for victims, to its current position as both a frontline service and a global leader in technological solutions like StopNCII.org. It explores how the Helpline has adapted to emerging threats, growing case numbers, and shifting public awareness—particularly in the wake of the COVID-19 pandemic, which intensified online abuse and revealed the systemic gaps in victim support. The chapter also reflects on how victim experiences, law enforcement responses, and platform accountability have (and have not) evolved over time. It is an introduction to the operation of the Helpline, its formation, and the ecosystem in which it exists. A number of themes introduced here will be explored in more detail in later chapters. However, this chapter frames the context and introduces these issues alongside the journey of the Helpline and its practitioners.

Crucially, this is not just a story about reactive support. It is a chronicle of activism, collaboration, and technological progress aimed at prevention, empowerment, and justice. As we mark a decade since its founding, this chapter serves as both a retrospective and a call to action: to recognize the enduring harms of intimate image abuse, to sustain and strengthen the ecosystems that support survivors, and to demand global, systemic change.

The Beginning

The founding of the Revenge Porn Helpline was announced by the UK Government (2015a) in February 2015, just before the Criminal Justice and Courts Act 2015, Section 33 (UK Government, 2015b—see Chapter 3) came into force in April that made it a criminal offence to share intimate images of someone without their consent with the intention to cause distress. But these events didn't come out of nowhere, they were a response to a growing awareness of the prevalence and devastating impact of this form of abuse. A BBC article[1] from 2014 outlined early instances that gained media attention: the recording leaked of Tulisa Contostavlos in 2012 (discussed in more detail in Chapter 4),[2] the rise and fall of Is Anyone Up? and Hunter Moore (Levendowski, 2013) and the 2014 celebrity nude iCloud leak known coarsely as the "fappening" (Massanari, 2017). But, as the BBC article shows, while cases involving celebrities hit the headlines, this was something that was happening to ordinary women everywhere; the Urban Dictionary's earliest definition of "revenge porn" as "[h]omemade porn uploaded by ex girlfriend or (usually) ex boyfriend after particularly vicious breakup as a means of humiliating the ex or just for own amusement"[3] dates from 2007.

In 2011, the charity SWGfL,[4] as part of the UK Safer Internet Centre,[5] launched the Professionals Online Safety Helpline (POSH)[6] as a pilot project focused on child online safety and to provide advice and support to professionals working with children. From its beginnings, POSH received disclosures from adults, particularly teachers who were victims of intimate image abuse. They reported images circulating around school communities: children, parents, and colleagues. Some were suspended, others lost their jobs as the focus rested on the victim's actions not those of the perpetrator. Other charities and support services began to get in touch for advice on handling cases and it became clear that there was no existing service equipped to address this growing issue.

As media interest increased, it became apparent that existing legislative frameworks around malicious communications, public disorder and harassment were difficult to apply to these cases (Phippen & Brennan, 2020). Advocacy efforts from the Helpline led to briefings in Parliament, but there was resistance to defining intimate image abuse as a

---

[1] https://www.bbc.co.uk/news/uk-england-30308942. Accessed May 2025.

[2] https://www.theguardian.com/culture/2012/jul/12/tulisa-contostavlos-apology-sex-tape. Accessed May 2025.

[3] https://www.urbandictionary.com/define.php?term=revenge%20porn. Accessed May 2025.

[4] http://www.swgfl.org.uk/. Accessed May 2025.

[5] https://saferinternet.org.uk/. Accessed May 2025.

[6] https://swgfl.org.uk/helplines/professionals-online-safety-helpline/. Accessed May 2025.

crime and discussions were often overshadowed by victim-blaming narratives. Crucial to overcoming these barriers was the support of MPs such as Maria Miller, who raised cases from her own constituency to drive her campaign that led to the introduction of Section 33. At the same time, it became clear that victims would need advice and support in this new landscape, in particular with the difficulties of having images removed from the internet. At SWGfL, the cause was championed by Laura Higgins, and as a result, the Revenge Porn Helpline was born, funded by the Government Equalities Office, initially as a one-year pilot.

At the beginning, we anticipated that the people who came to the Helpline would be experiencing the issues that Government had legislated for: callers would be predominantly female, images would be shared by predominantly male former partners and the images would have been uploaded, for maximum impact, to social media sites such as Facebook, Twitter and Instagram and the major adult platforms such as Pornhub and xHamster. We aimed to explain the law as it applied to people's experiences, encourage people to report to the police and remove the images that were reported to us. But, while much of this is what happened, we soon realized that the reality of people's experiences was more complex and our response would need to be nuanced. We learned to manage people's expectations about reporting to the police to achieve justice; we found that images were being shared for many more reasons than disgruntled ex-partners lashing out; and we realized that the initial sharing of an image on Facebook or Pornhub was just the start.

The Helpline ran alongside POSH from the beginning, as it does to this day, sharing experience and building on SWGfL's long-standing relationships with the tech industry to achieve swift and efficient outcomes for victims. Initially, platforms had vague or non-existent policies for non-consensual intimate images, with some even promoting their spread due to their popularity. In time, platform policies improved but enforcement was inconsistent. Ten years later, many platforms have dedicated trusted flagger reporting routes and portals but this is by no means universal.

Another crucial development in this space in 2015 was the establishment of SPITE[7] as part of the Legal Advice Centre at Queen Mary University of London. SPITE (Sharing and Publishing Images To Embarrass) is the only law clinic providing specialist free legal advice to victims of intimate image abuse. This resource is vital for victims of this abuse, since they are often experiencing overlapping issues in a complex and evolving legal area. The Revenge Porn Helpline and SPITE established early on the means to cross-refer to ensure that victims received all the appropriate support and advice available.

The evaluation of the pilot year (Bond & Dogaru, 2019) demonstrated the need for the service, but also identified the themes that would stay current in the following years. Women made up the majority of victims calling the Helpline at 79% with 19% identifying as male, however sextortion was an issue that came to the fore early with 12% of cases in the first year with men most likely to be victims. Early on there were instances of "fake" images, created predominantly by using digital editing tools such as Adobe Photoshop, which were usually crude and unconvincing but still caused the harm and distress that was intended and was a dark precursor to the rise of AI-generated "deepfakes" that we have seen since (Šepec & Lango, 2020). Also common were so-called "tribute" pages, where non-intimate images of named women were sexualized by the addition of penises and/or semen (Lumsden & Morgan, 2018).

One of the earliest activities of the Helpline, beyond the immediate needs of people seeking support, was engaging with other support services. It was clear that many of the people reporting intimate image abuse were experiencing other forms of abuse and needed additional support. We were regularly signposting to domestic abuse services as well as stalking services and charities offering support to members of particular communities such as LGBTQ+ or specific religious groups. However, engagement with some of the major charities in these spaces was difficult initially as understanding of the connections between online and offline abusive behaviours was in its infancy. Similarly, the Helpline

[7] https://www.qmul.ac.uk/lac/clients/advice/revenge-porn-free-legal-advice/.

struggled to engage with policing to support with the training of officers to improve criminal justice system outcomes. Research by one of this book's authors (Bond & Tyrrell, 2021) found that 94.7% of police respondents had not received any training on how to investigate these cases, and of those that did have some training, it was felt to be of limited use.

People coming to the Helpline have always reported disappointing interactions with the police, both frontline officers and call handlers. The evaluation of the first year reported "victims had rather mixed but often poor experiences when they contacted the police", with one person saying: "The woman who has dealt with me has said that they have never dealt with this before, but they know how bad it is and how much distress it's causing me. But they are totally clueless about this kind of crime, and I mean that in a nice way. I'm not saying I will, but what if I committed suicide tonight? They have done absolutely nothing to help this". Lack of training in investigating online offending has been a constant theme of the last ten years. While more understandable in 2015, there has been limited change. But as damaging as an inability to investigate effectively is, equally so are the victim-blaming narratives that are expressed by officers. The phrases "why did you take the picture in the first place?" and "what did you think was going to happen when you sent it?" were common in 2015 but are still being said in 2025. More empathetic officers still struggled to advise victims on how they could have images removed, lacking knowledge about existing law enforcement routes to social media platforms and failing to signpost to the Revenge Porn Helpline. Early on it became clear that police involvement, or even a prosecution, would not lead to the removal of online content, one client reporting: "Even after the police were involved and the photos removed he has continued to post the same videos with my full name as well as degrading captions all over the internet". In this context, it is not surprising that the numbers of convictions were low: in 2015–16, the CPS reported 206 convictions,[8] rising to 465 in 2016–17,[9] 464 in 2017–18[10] and falling to 376 in 2018–19.[11]

The first thing that every person who comes to the Helpline asks, if they have had images shared of them online, is a version of "get my images down". The request is understandably urgent and desperate to stop their most private and intimate moments being seen by friends, family and work colleagues. While not an emergency service, we do our best to report images quickly, but almost inevitably, images shared on one website or platform by a perpetrator will be quickly shared onwards by third parties or downloaded for personal use and potentially later sharing. What this means is that one intimate image of a person can swiftly become 10, or a hundred. And if there are multiple images, they can proliferate in albums across adult sites, dedicated message boards and file-sharing services in days or hours. Initial sharing often happened on the major social media and adult sites, but subsequent sharings would move the images further from the centre to less legitimate sites or those dedicated to non-consensual content. For these secondary sharings, the intention was not about causing distress to the victim at all (and therefore fell outside the criminal definition) but simply about the trading and collection of this content for its own sake. The Helpline decided very early on that it was not enough to simply report the images for removal that victims/survivors asked us to: we would need to search for and report additional instances of the images. And it is this that tests the capacity of the Helpline: the nature of the internet and the nature of the behaviour that shares and reshares images means that this is a never-ending task. Even if the Helpline manages to achieve a 100% takedown rate for someone, it is always possible that someone has downloaded the images and will upload them anew one day for their own and their peers' gratification. And this knowledge will have the greatest impact on victims, as they know that they can never be guaranteed freedom from the circulation of their intimate images.

8 https://www.cps.gov.uk/sites/default/files/documents/publications/cps_vawg_report_2016.pdf.

9 https://www.cps.gov.uk/sites/default/files/documents/publications/cps-vawg-report-2017_0.pdf.

10 https://www.cps.gov.uk/sites/default/files/documents/publications/cps-vawg-report-2018.pdf.

11 https://www.cps.gov.uk/sites/default/files/documents/publications/cps-vawg-report-2019.pdf.

2020: The Pandemic Impact

At the end of 2019, the Law Commission (2018) announced that they had been commissioned by government to conduct an inquiry into the taking, making and sharing of intimate images without consent following their scoping report on Abusive and Offensive Online Communications. The Revenge Porn Helpline and other stakeholders welcomed the new review as an essential step in assessing responses to intimate image abuse from the criminal justice system with an expectation of recommendations on legislative change. As a key stakeholder in this space, the Helpline gave early evidence to the Inquiry and engaged in multiple stakeholder roundtables and evidence sessions. However, the Inquiry's progress stalled as the world order changed in March 2020 with the spread of COVID-19 and lockdowns in the UK and worldwide.

At the time of the first UK lockdown, the Helpline was just into its sixth year and was staffed by three people: myself (Sophie Mortimer) and practitioners Kate Worthington and Zara Ward. In mid-March, the decision had been taken that we would work from home, with the expectation that it wouldn't last more than a few weeks. In the end, we did not return to the office until June 2020, and then on a limited basis.

The lockdown entirely changed the way the Helpline operated: the phone line was closed and we relied on email and our anonymous Whisper tool; and Kate and Zara were unable to view or report online content to protect their wellbeing. When necessary, I checked links that were submitted by clients and these were then reported, but we could do no additional searches. For the first few weeks of the lockdown, the Helpline was eerily quiet. In 2019, we had seen an average of 140 cases per month which was starting to rise in early 2020 to 170, but that April a floodgate cracked open. Case numbers rose to 240, 280 and by the end of 2020 they were over 300 per month. Some months of 2021 went over 400 cases.

There seemed to be multiple reasons for the increase: so much of people's lives had shifted online for work, entertainment and maintaining personal connections; the ability to interact online grew faster than the measures to keep people safe once they were online. The criminal gangs operating sextortion schemes suddenly had enormous captive audiences, trapped in their own homes with only their devices to access company. People in abusive and controlling relationships were caught in a pressure cooker, where threats and abuse could spiral; and former partners suddenly had time on their hands to inflict pain. And it wasn't just the Revenge Porn Helpline: services across the country supporting victims of abuse reported increases: the National Domestic Abuse Helpline reported a 65% increase in calls between April and June 2020, a 12% increase in demand for domestic abuse support when lockdown restrictions first eased[12] and an increase in more complex cases including sixteen fatal domestic homicides in the first three weeks of lockdown, the highest level for over 11 years.[13]

Government responded swiftly to the wealth of evidence and accompanying media coverage[14] and additional funding was made available to VAWG (Violence Against Women and Girls) services, including the Revenge Porn Helpline. We were able to recruit an additional practitioner and when we were allowed back into the office, the team worked hard to catch up on the backlog of content reporting. The additional funding continued into 2021 when we were able to recruit a further two practitioners, building capacity to give effective support to the increasing numbers of people coming to us for help.

Threats to Share

As discussed in more detail in the following chapters where we explore the law in more depth, the initial legislation was severely lacking regarding considering threats to share. In July 2020, the domestic abuse charity Refuge launched a campaign called "The Naked Threat"[15] which called on the government to make the threat to share intimate images

---

[12] https://www.ons.gov.uk/peoplepopulationandcommunity/crimeandjustice/bulletins/domesticabuseinenglandandwalesoverview/november2020. Accessed May 2025.

[13] https://commonslibrary.parliament.uk/domestic-abuse-and-covid-19-A-year-into-the-pandemic/.. Accessed May 2025.

[14] https://www.bbc.co.uk/news/stories-52413994. Accessed May 2025.

[15] https://refuge.org.uk/news/refuge-launches-the-naked-threat-campaign/. Accessed May 2025.

without consent a criminal offence. Excluded from the original legislation, Refuge had seen a rise in the use of threats to share intimate images by perpetrators to intimidate and control victims. Their survey found that 1 in 14 adults in England and Wales had experienced such threats, rising to 1 in 7 of young women aged 18–34. After a vigorous campaign from Refuge, supported by both the Domestic Abuse and Victims' Commissioners, and a high-profile media campaign, the government responded by adding threats to share intimate images to the existing legislation via the Domestic Abuse Act in 2021 (UK Government, 2021).

National Crime Agency

Another event that changed significantly the way the Helpline operated at this time was our work with the National Crime Agency (NCA). We had shared information regarding sextortion from the beginning, but in April 2019, the NCA came to us about a specific case. To protect the victims/survivors I will give limited details about the case here: however, it involved a prolific offender who was being investigated and was finally arrested that year. The NCA asked us to support them with the removal of related images as far as was possible to minimize the impact on those affected. However, by this time, many of the images had been available online for months and were appearing on some of the hardest sites to engage with.

In October 2020, the NCA shared the information that they had to enable us to identify the victim/survivors and their images. The team started the gruelling task of searching for the thousands of images available of dozens of women. These images were not only widespread on multiple sites that specialized in extreme content, but the content itself was some of the most graphic that the Helpline has ever seen. The systematic process of finding and reporting these images began in 2020 but continues to this day as the images continue to circulate. At the time of writing (April 2025), the total number of images reported relating to this case is over 215,000 with a removal rate of 96%. The Helpline will continue to search for and report images for the foreseeable future.

Comic Relief

As numbers continued to rise throughout 2021 it became clear that, despite additional government funding, we would need to explore other ways to provide support to victims of abuse. Our data showed that 60% of the people contacting the Helpline were coming to us outside of the Helpline's operational hours. And while we had worked to ensure that the Helpline website contained the necessary information, we knew that there was so much there that it would be difficult to navigate, particularly in a state of distress and anxiety. We decided that a cost-effective solution would be a chatbot to guide users around the website and get them the advice they would need as quickly as possible.

We applied for, and were successful in achieving, funding from Comic Relief's Tech for Good fund and they gave support throughout the discover, design and delivery stages of the process. In February 2022, the chatbot, Reiya, went live on the Helpline's website and within weeks was running over 500 unique sessions per month. This has now tripled and over 50 sessions are run every day. Reiya guides people through the website for the advice they need and has been incredibly successful in triaging people to the right place: victims of sextortion can get the immediate advice to stop, block and report; young people under the age of 18 can get prompt signposting to the IWF, Report Remove or support services like The Mix; and people outside the UK are directed to a list of overseas services. Reiya has ensured that people we are unable to help can get what they need elsewhere as quickly as possible and has allowed the Helpline team to prioritize UK adults we are best suited to help.

StopNCII.org

In 2017, Facebook launched a pilot project called Not Without My Consent,[16] which was intended to build upon their own internal systems designed to prevent the resharing of intimate images without consent.

---

16 https://about.fb.com/wp-content/uploads/2017/03/not-without-my-consent.pdf. Accessed May 2025.

This was done through the application of a technology known as "digital fingerprinting" or hashing, which is the industry standard used widely to stop the spread of child sexual abuse material (CSAM) online. In simple terms, a hash is a unique piece of code that represents a photograph or video and which can used to find duplicates. Facebook had been using this technology internally: if they removed a non-consensual intimate image (NCII) they created a hash of the image, which they would then store to compare against uploaded images to identify and block matches.

Not Without My Consent aimed to give people being threatened with the sharing of their images the opportunity to *pre-emptively* create hashes of them that could be used by Facebook to stop them being shared on the platform at all. A revolutionary idea in this area, the logistics created barriers: someone wanting to create hashes of their images needed to be referred by a service in their country. In the UK, that was the Revenge Porn Helpline, but most of the world did not have a service that would be able to make these referrals. Secondly, the hashes would only be shared to Facebook and Instagram while the problem was much, much larger. And thirdly, and the biggest barrier of all, was that people would have to send their intimate images to Facebook via an upload link for them to create the hashes. In the wake of disclosures about Facebook's use of data and privacy concerns, the credibility of the new programme was damaged. But then a new idea emerged.

In late 2020, Facebook, or Meta as they became in 2021, approached SWGfL and the Revenge Porn Helpline to propose that we worked together to build a more victim-centric evolution of Not Without My Consent. The premise was simple: to create a new platform that would create the hashes that would stop the spread of NCII with three important differences. Firstly, it would be available directly from people's own devices: no referrals would be needed and there would be no need to send images anywhere as the hashes were created on the person's *own device*. Secondly, the platform would be available to any adult anywhere in the world, immediately. And, thirdly, hashes could be shared with multiple platforms, not just Facebook and Instagram. The Helpline team, Meta and an independent engineering team worked on the project throughout

2021 and StopNCII.org[17] launched that December with Facebook and Instagram as founding partners. Three years later and a dozen of the major global platforms have joined the initiative to protect people from becoming victims of intimate image abuse, with more partners in the process of joining; the hashes are protecting well over a million images and nearly 30,000 images have been blocked.

StopNCII.org, as a preventative technology, is a gamechanger in this space. It has the potential to offer realistic protections to adults around the world so that they will never become victims of this abuse. But the challenge that exists is to ensure that the hashes are applied everywhere: there are thousands of websites around the world that will support the resharing of NCII and it will take a global effort of legislation, regulation and enforcement to make it happen.

2023–25: At the Time of Writing

As we approached the tenth anniversary of the founding of the Helpline in 2025, we began to plan a campaign[18] that reflected on how far we had come, where we are now, and how much there is still to do to give victims and survivors the just outcomes they deserve. The behaviours that abusers deploy to cause pain have not really changed since 2015, but we understand them better; at the same time, the numbers of platforms and tools and technological developments have grown exponentially. And while our responses have improved, we need to focus on prevention if we want to dramatically reduce the harms caused by intimate image abuse.

Women still come to the Helpline more often than men, but they each experience intimate image abuse differently. Men, predominantly, experience sextortion and to a lesser extent the sharing of images by former partners. Women most commonly experience the sharing of intimate images and threats to share by current or former partners and men

[17] https://stopncii.org/. Accessed May 2025.

[18] https://swgfl.org.uk/magazine/intimate-image-abuse-is-not-going-away-10-years-of-the-revenge-porn-helpline/. Accessed May 2025.

who are known to them; but women also have images saved, shared, and reshared by strangers who collect and trade images with peers on dedicated sites and message boards. In fact, over 98% of the intimate images that the Helpline has reported in the last ten years, have been of women.

Women still frequently experience victim-blaming from the people closest to them when they disclose, or when they report what has happened to the police making it harder for them to support investigations and prosecutions and reducing the likelihood of other women reporting at all. The cycle becomes self-perpetuating as women are discouraged from meaningful protest about their abuse, so perpetrators become more confident in their entitlement to do as they choose and the protective systems fail to recognize and engage with the seriousness of the abuse and the impact on victims. Women who have intimate images shared of them are left carrying the blame and shame of what has happened and no options that won't make their situation worse than it already is.

There have been some improvements in recent years that we hope will start to bring change. Government accepted the recommendations of the thorough inquiry by the Law Commission which published its report in 2022[19] and planned legislation that would replace wholesale the existing Section 33 of the Criminal Justice and Courts Act 2015 (ibid.). The new legislation would make it a criminal offence to share intimate images, regardless of any motivation or none, it broadened the definition of an intimate image to include partially nude and synthetic images and guaranteed anonymity to victims. The new offences were added to the Sexual Offences Act 2003 via the Online Safety Act (2023) and came into effect in January 2024; they were also added to the list of priority offences that Ofcom will be mandated to ensure platforms act on when the new OSA regime comes into effect in 2025.

Helpline responses to clients have adapted and strengthened as the Helpline has become more experienced and as capacity has increased. Policies and processes are regularly reviewed to ensure we are giving the

---

[19] https://webarchive.nationalarchives.gov.uk/ukgwa/20250109101427mp_/https://cloud-platform-e218f50a4812967ba1215eaecede923f.s3.amazonaws.com/uploads/sites/30/2022/07/Intimate-image-abuse-final-report.pdf. Accessed May 2025.

best service to the people that come to us; the chatbot supports practitioners to focus their time where it's most needed, and there are more tools available to aid searching and reporting of images for removal.

The ecosystem of support for victims and survivors has evolved too: the Helpline has developed close relationships with other services across the UK VAWG sector to share training and learning, track trends and provide comprehensive support. We collaborate on campaigns, awareness-raising and lobbying government for further change. We have all been supported by powerful activists such as Jodie Campaigns,[20] #NotYourPorn[21] and My Image My Choice.[22] It is vital that these voices continue to work together to pursue shared goals that will reduce the harms of this abuse and improve outcomes for victims.

Intimate image abuse is an issue that crosses jurisdictional boundaries and there has been improved collaboration between countries in recent years. The Biden administration in the USA established the White House Task Force to Address Online Harassment and Abuse in 2022 (White House, 2023) that aimed to improve responses to a range of online issues including IIA, by requiring better, faster actions from industry and attempting to guide the development of AI safely. At the same time, it looks likely that the USA will pass federal legislation this year that, alongside federal offences of sharing intimate images without consent, will create mandatory requirements on platforms to remove content in 48 hours.

The United Nations have been developing a new Cybercrime Convention that is expected to pass this year (United Nations, 2024); Article 16 will require all member states to have legislation that criminalizes the sharing of intimate images without consent. The Helpline has conducted a mapping exercise[23] to determine how many countries are compliant with the new legislation which demonstrates that there is still much work to do but we anticipate the Convention will provide the momentum needed.

---

[20] https://www.bbc.co.uk/news/uk-68673390. Accessed May 2025.

[21] https://notyourporn.com/. Accessed May 2025.

[22] https://myimagemychoice.org/. Accessed May 2025.

[23] https://swgfl.org.uk/resources/adult-image-based-abuse-model-response/. Accessed May 2025.

Our own platform, StopNCII.org, has continued to add industry partners and establish a pipeline to keep the numbers building. At the same time, we have developed a network of over 100 NGOs[24] around the world that provide support to IIA victims, sharing experience and learning of how this abuse manifests in different cultures and communities globally. We make sure that they have up-to-date information on developments and campaigns and input their knowledge into plans for the development of StopNCII.org, because the tool has to work for everyone.

As the following chapters outline, there is still much to do to improve support for victims, across Helpline services, legislation, tech platforms, policing and the wider criminal justice system. To date, much of the focus on online safety has, understandably, been focused on children, but it is past time that attention was paid to the harms experienced by adults too. We need comprehensive support across all age groups that is accessible and appropriate regardless of age, ethnicity or background. An ecosystem of support needs to be established that operates globally to reflect the borderless nature of the internet; with stable multi-year funding that allows for the development of solutions and agile responses to an evolving landscape. And while we need to create a shift in cultural attitudes, this needs to start with dedicated research to understand perpetration so resources can be focused for maximum effect, target deterrence messaging at potential offenders, challenge existing narratives and reduce the stigma of this abuse. The remainder of this book conducts this research and considers the future of the Helpline, how learning can be projected in a global context, and what else needs to be done.

References

Bond, E., & Dogaru, C. (2019). *Evaluation of the Pilot Project*. https://revengepornhelpline.org.uk/assets/documents/evaluation-pilot-project-2016.pdf. Accessed May 2025.

[24] https://stopncii.org/partners/global-network-of-partners/.

Bond, E., & Tyrrell, K. (2021). Understanding revenge pornography: A national survey of police officers and staff in England and Wales. *Journal of Interpersonal Violence, 36*(5–6), 2166–2181.

Law Commission. (2018). *Abusive and Offensive Online Communications: A Scoping Report*. https://www.gov.uk/government/publications/abusive-and-offensive-online-communications-a-scoping-report. Accessed May 2025.

Levendowski, A. (2013). Using copyright to combat revenge porn. *NYU Journal of Intellectual Property & Entertainment Law, 3*, 422.

Lumsden, K., & Morgan, H. M. (2018). Cyber-trolling as symbolic violence: Deconstructing gendered abuse online. In *The Routledge handbook of gender and violence* (pp. 121–132). Routledge.

Massanari, A. (2017). # Gamergate and The Fappening: How Reddit's algorithm, governance, and culture support toxic technocultures. *New Media & Society, 19*(3), 329–346.

Phippen, A., & Brennan, M. (2020). *Sexting and revenge pornography: Legislative and social dimensions of a modern digital phenomenon*. Routledge.

Šepec, M., & Lango, M. (2020). Virtual revenge pornography as a new online threat to sexual integrity. *Balkan Social Science Review, 15*, 117–135.

The White House. (2023). *White House Task Force to Address Online Harassment and Abuse Blueprint and Final Report*. https://bidenwhitehouse.archives.gov/wp-content/uploads/2024/05/White-House-Task-Force-to-Address-Online-Harassment-and-Abuse_FINAL.pdf. Accessed May 2025.

UK Government. (2015a). *Revenge porn helpline launched by government*. https://www.gov.uk/government/news/revenge-porn-helpline-launched-by-government. Accessed May 2025.

UK Government. (2015b). *Criminal Justice and Courts Act 2015, c. 2, § 33*. https://www.legislation.gov.uk/ukpga/2015/2/section/33. Accessed May 2025.

UK Government. (2021). *Domestic Abuse Act 2021: Section 69*. Legislation.gov.uk. https://www.legislation.gov.uk/ukpga/2021/17/section/69/enacted. Accessed May 2025.

UK Government. (2023). *Online Safety Act 2023*. https://www.legislation.gov.uk/ukpga/2023/50. Accessed May 2025.

United Nations. (2024). *United Nations Convention against Cybercrime: Strengthening international cooperation for combating certain crimes committed by means of information and communications technology systems and for the sharing of evidence in electronic form of serious crimes* (A/RES/79/243). https://documents.un.org/access.nsf/get?DS=A%2FRES%2F79%2F243&Lang=E. Accessed May 2025.

3

Intimate Image Abuse Law and Policy in the UK

Abstract This chapter offers a comprehensive legal analysis of the evolution of UK legislation addressing Intimate Image Abuse (IIA), from its early reliance on outdated civil and criminal statutes to the creation of specific offences under the *Criminal Justice and Courts Act 2015* and subsequent reforms in the *Domestic Abuse Act 2021* and *Online Safety Act 2023.* It critically examines how early laws failed to account for coercion, synthetic images, threats to share, and non-sexual but intimate imagery, limiting protection for victims. Drawing on landmark cases and historical precedents, the chapter contextualizes the emergence of IIA as a legal issue shaped by societal double standards, digital innovation, and victim advocacy. Central to the chapter is the pivotal role of the Revenge Porn Helpline (RPH), whose frontline data and casework directly influenced major policy changes and shaped the national response. By highlighting disparities across UK jurisdictions and ongoing gaps—such as inconsistent definitions, lack of anonymity, and inadequate law enforcement training—the chapter calls for a unified, victim-centred legal framework that foregrounds consent over perpetrator intent and integrates technological and cultural responses to digital sexual harm.

S. Mortimer et al., *Ten Years of the Revenge Porn Helpline*, Palgrave Studies in Victims and Victimology, https://doi.org/10.1007/978-3-032-00614-1_3

Keywords Intimate Image Abuse (IIA) · Criminal Justice and Courts Act 2015 · Revenge Porn Helpline · Deepfakes and synthetic media · Online safety legislation

The Revenge Porn Helpline took its first cases in February 2015, two months ahead of the legislation making it a criminal offence to share intimate images without consent. In the ten years since then there has been much change in our understanding of the issue and the legal responses to improve support for victims. The legislation as first envisaged was attempting to tackle cases of private sexual images, taken consensually in the first instance, but then shared by one party to cause direct harm to the other. This framing influenced how the legislation was structured, what was included and what was excluded. As we will see, this approach meant that many uses of intimate images that caused harm fell outside the scope of the law and revealed quite quickly that it was not fit for purpose.

This chapter traces the development of legal responses to IIA in the UK, from early privacy and harassment cases brought through civil courts, to the landmark Criminal Justice and Courts Act 2015 (UK Government, 2015), and the more comprehensive reforms introduced in the Domestic Abuse Act 2021 (UK Government, 2021) and Online Safety Act 2023 (UK Government, 2023). It explores how initial laws, while symbolically important, failed to fully account for the range of abusive behaviours victims experienced—including coercive threats, synthetic images, and digitally manipulated content. The chapter also highlights the inconsistent and evolving legal approaches across the UK's devolved jurisdictions.

Central to this legal evolution has been the work of the Revenge Porn Helpline. Established just prior to the introduction of the 2015 legislation, the Helpline has played a pivotal role not only in directly supporting victims, but also in identifying legislative gaps, informing public discourse, and providing crucial evidence to policymakers. Its case data and frontline insights have shaped both public understanding and legislative reform, contributing directly to key legal changes such as the criminalization of threats to share, the inclusion of deepfakes, and the removal of intent-to-cause-distress requirements.

This chapter begins by situating IIA within a longer history of non-consensual image use, predating digital technology, before moving through landmark legal cases, political debates, and the incremental reforms that have gradually built a more coherent legislative framework. Throughout, the chapter underscores how law has both responded to, and been challenged by, the lived experiences of victims and how front-line support services like the RPH have helped bridge the gap between abstract legal principles and real-world harm.

A Brief History of Image-Based Abuse

Although legal frameworks addressing image-based abuse are relatively new, the underlying acts of non-consensual image sharing have existed long before the advent of technology that enabled the easy creation and distribution of intimate images.

While camera phones have only been around for about two decades, the misuse of intimate images for extortion, control, and financial gain predates the digital era. The introduction of instant cameras in the 1940s, particularly Polaroids, allowed individuals to take intimate photographs without the risk of public exposure at a commercial photo development studio. However, these images were still exploited for manipulation. The most notable early example was the 1963 divorce case of the Duke and Duchess of Argyll (Dickie, 1966), where explicit Polaroid photographs played a central role, even becoming the subject of a government investigation decades later.

This case stemmed from the 1963 divorce proceedings between Margaret Campbell, the Duchess of Argyll, and Ian Campbell, the 11th Duke of Argyll. Their marriage had been troubled, with accusations of infidelity and financial struggles. During the divorce, the Duke produced stolen explicit photographs and letters of Margaret, including a now-infamous Polaroid of her performing oral sex on an unidentified "Headless Man". This evidence was used against her in court, leading to a high profile and very public trial.

The blackmail aspect of the case relates to how these materials were obtained and used. Margaret maintained that her private documents were stolen from her residence, and this was likely orchestrated by her husband. Some of the men linked to her—including politicians and aristocrats—were rumoured to have been blackmailed or pressured to stay silent. The judge in the case shamed Margaret publicly, calling her "completely promiscuous" and denying her any financial support, while the men involved faced little to no consequences.

The scandal ruined the Duchess's reputation, and she was ostracized from high society. Despite the humiliation, she remained defiant and refused to express regret for her private life. Over time, the case became a symbol of hypocrisy and double standards in Britain's aristocratic circles, where male infidelity was overlooked but women's sexuality was harshly condemned (Castle, 2021). The identity of the "Headless Man", which remains one of Britain's great unsolved mysteries, adding to the case's enduring intrigue and public interest.

Beyond high-profile scandals, the non-consensual sharing of intimate images also surfaced in the 1980s through publications like US adult magazine Hustler's "Beaver Hunt" feature (Kipnis, 2013). In this section of the publication, readers submitted intimate images—sometimes of themselves, sometimes of others—along with personal details. Lawsuits emerged when individuals claimed their images had been published without consent, often with forged consent forms, highlighting early legal battles over privacy, copyright, and negligence in verifying submissions (Bustamante, 2016). The financial incentives for fraudulent submissions, with Hustler offering $50 per image, underscored the exploitative nature of the practice.

While these early examples of what we would now refer to as NCII or IIA highlight both the use of non-consensual imagery in abuse long before digital technology made the production and distribution of media far easier, they are still rooted in concerns about privacy, control, and exploitation that have beset more modern cases which, ultimately, contributed to the development of legislation specifically to address the harms caused by IIA. Prior to the implementation of specific criminal law to address these issues, civil law has also played a crucial role in preventing the distribution of private images.

Publishing private images without consent can lead to civil suits for breach of confidence or privacy violations if the subject had a reasonable expectation of privacy. Unless there is a public interest justification, such as exposing hypocrisy in a public figure, the legal system offers few defences for non-consensual disclosure (Pollack, 2016).

A foundational and influential case that was used in cases more explicitly related to the issues of IIA was that of *Campbell v MGN Ltd* [2004] UKHL 22.[1] Centring on privacy rights, this landmark decision in UK law helped establish the modern framework for misuse of private information (Lintern-Davies & Doherty, 2006). It arose when *Mirror Group Newspapers* (*MGN*) published an article revealing that Naomi Campbell, a then internationally famous celebrity, was attending Narcotics Anonymous (NA) meetings. The article included specific details about her treatment, along with photographs of her leaving a meeting. Campbell, who had previously denied using drugs in public statements, sued *MGN*, arguing that the publication was a breach of confidence and an invasion of her privacy.

At the heart of the legal dispute was the question of whether the article and accompanying photographs constituted a misuse of private information. *MGN* defended its publication on the grounds of public interest, claiming that since Campbell had misled the public about her drug use, the newspaper had a right to expose the truth. The case also raised fundamental questions about the balance between privacy rights (Article 8 of the European Convention on Human Rights) and press freedom (Article 10 of the Convention).

In a 3-2 majority ruling (ibid.), the House of Lords found in favour of Campbell. The court acknowledged that because she had previously denied taking drugs, her drug use itself was a legitimate matter of public interest. However, it concluded that the specific details of her medical treatment, including the fact that she was attending NA meetings, were not necessary to correct the public record. The publication of this private information, particularly the photographs, was deemed an unwarranted intrusion into her personal life. The ruling emphasized that even public

[1] https://publications.parliament.uk/pa/ld200304/ldjudgmt/jd040506/campbe-1.htm.

figures are entitled to privacy, especially concerning medical treatment and mental health.

Ultimately, this case shaped the modern approach to privacy law in the UK, defining the limits of media intrusion into the private lives of public figures. While it reaffirmed the press's role in holding individuals accountable, it also placed necessary restrictions on the extent to which personal details be exposed in the name of public interest. It has subsequently been used in other civil cases more closely related to IIA.

AMP v Persons Unknown is a notable 2011 case in the UK where the High Court addressed issues of privacy and harassment in the digital age.[2] The claimant, referred to as AMP to maintain anonymity, lost her mobile phone in June 2008 while at university. The device contained explicit images taken for personal use. Subsequently, these images were uploaded online without her consent, leading to blackmail attempts and significant distress.

A crucial element of this case was its reliance on privacy law, particularly under Article 8 of the European Convention on Human Rights (ECHR). This provision guarantees an individual's right to a private and family life, which the Human Rights Act 1998 enshrines in UK law. The court found that the unauthorized dissemination of AMP's private images constituted a grave violation of this right. Unlike cases where public interest might justify publication, there was no legitimate reason for sharing such intimate material. The ruling reaffirmed the principle established in earlier privacy cases, such as *Campbell v MGN Ltd* (2004), that privacy rights could override the right to freedom of expression when personal and sensitive information was at stake.

In addition to privacy law, AMP's case involved the Protection from Harassment Act 1997 (UK Government, 1997), a statute traditionally used to combat stalking and persistent abuse. Given that AMP had been subjected to blackmail attempts linked to the leaked images, the court recognized that this constituted harassment under the Act. The distress caused by the threats and ongoing exposure underscored the necessity of urgent judicial intervention, reinforcing the need for an injunction to prevent further harm.

---

[2] https://www.bailii.org/ew/cases/EWHC/TCC/2011/3454.html. Accessed May 2025.

Furthermore, AMP's claim cited *breach of confidence*, a legal principle designed to protect information shared in confidence from unauthorized disclosure. Since the images in question were taken for personal use and never intended for public dissemination, their unauthorized publication amounted to a clear breach of confidence. The court upheld this argument, emphasizing that individuals retain a reasonable expectation of privacy over their private images, even in the digital realm.

By grounding its decision in these legal principles, the High Court underscored the growing need for robust legal protections in an era where digital content can be widely disseminated with ease and without consent. This case served as an important precedent in shaping the legal response to online privacy violations and unauthorized content distribution (Brimblecombe & Fenwick, 2022). It is also significant as it marked the first instance where a UK court issued an injunction against unknown individuals to prevent the distribution of specific content online.

As introduced in Chapter 2, *Contostavlos v Mendahun* [2012] EWHC 850 (QB) (Agate & Ledward, 2013) is a landmark case in UK privacy law, and one that attracted considerable public attention at the time, as it involved British singer and television personality Tulisa Contostavlos. The case centred on the unauthorized dissemination of a private video depicting Contostavlos engaged in sexual activity with her former boyfriend, Justin Edwards.

In August 2011, Contostavlos was informed by *The Sun* newspaper about an attempt to sell footage allegedly showing her in a sexual act. At that time, she had not seen the footage and did not recall its creation, leading her public relations representative to publicly deny its authenticity. However, in March 2012, the video was posted on various websites, including one operated by the first defendant, Michael Mendahun. Upon viewing the footage, Contostavlos confirmed its authenticity and expressed distress over its publication, accusing Edwards of making it public without consent.

Contostavlos sought an interim injunction to prevent further dissemination of the video. The High Court granted the injunction against the defendants, including *persons unknown* who might possess or control the footage. The court recognized that details of an individual's sexual life are highly private and warrant protection from public disclosure. The judge noted that photographs and videos are particularly intrusive, and the unauthorized dissemination of such intimate material has little to no prospect of being defensible under claims of public interest or public domain (Hughes, 2014).

The injunction was continued until trial or further order, effectively prohibiting the publication or disclosure of any film or video depicting Contostavlos engaged in sexual activity. The case highlighted the challenges posed by digital media in safeguarding personal privacy and set a precedent for similar cases involving the unauthorized distribution of private material.

Political Interest in Non-Consensual Intimate Images

These early cases highlighted the challenges victims faced in getting legal recourse because of IIA. In each case the victims have required considerable legal effort and argument, and undoubtedly expense, to address something that, from a moral perspective, should be straightforward—someone should not be able to take intimate images for another without consent and distribute them further. This does not seem to be too contentious a moral point, but it is one that the law, and policy makers, did struggle with prior to the introduction of the Criminal Justice and Courts Act 2015.

Within the Westminster parliament, the first mention of the rather problematic term "Revenge Pornography" took place in January 2014 during a debate about Cyberbullying, and it is interesting to note that, at the time, there was a view that current laws were sufficient[3]:

Dr Sarah Wollaston
(Totnes) (Con)

[3] https://hansard.parliament.uk/Commons/2014-01-27/debates/14012711000019/Cyber-Bullying#contribution-14012711000065.

5. What steps she is taking to prevent harassment through the sending of unsolicited sexual images via the internet and telephone.

The Minister for Crime Prevention
(Norman Baker)
The coalition Government takes all forms of harassment, whether online or offline, very seriously. We have robust legislation in place to deal with cyber-stalking and harassment, and perpetrators of grossly offensive, obscene or menacing behaviour face stiff punishment. We will continue to work collaboratively with industry, charities and parenting groups to develop tools and information for users aimed at keeping society safe online.

With the minister going on to state that[4]:

There are numerous pieces of legislation that they can use including, for example, the Malicious Communications Act 1988, under which it is an offence to send communications or other articles with intent to cause distress or anxiety.

We should at this stage also note that, even back in these early discussions, that this was considered more of an educational, rather than criminal, issue.[5]

Helen Jones
(Warrington North) (Lab)
But online or offline, the Minister knows that the best way of tackling abuse and violence against women is to have compulsory sex and relationship education in schools, which teaches our children about healthy and respectful relationships. Now that this is supported by the vast majority of parents and teachers, the NSPCC, mumsnet, the girl guides-all those who work in the sector dealing with violence against women-will the Government abandon their attempts to stop it and support the amendment in the Lords that would introduce this in our schools?
Norman Baker

---

[4] https://hansard.parliament.uk/Commons/2014-01-27/debates/14012711000019/Cyber-Bullying#contribution-14012711000070.

[5] https://hansard.parliament.uk/Commons/2014-01-27/debates/14012711000019/Cyber-Bullying#contribution-14012711000071.

> *Of course, that is predominantly a matter for the Department of Education than for the Home Office. I have discussed the matter with my colleagues in the DFE, but it is worth pointing out that 96% of primary schools and 73% of secondary schools teach e-safety, either as separate lessons or embedded in others*

Certainly, it is fair to say that there were several pieces of criminal law that could, in certain circumstances, be applied to issues related to IIA. For example:

- Malicious Communications Act 1988: Criminalized sending offensive, obscene, or threatening messages (UK Government, 1988).
- Communications Act 2003: Addressed grossly offensive or menacing electronic communications (UK Government, 2003).
- Protection from Harassment Act 1997: Applied when non-consensual sharing was part of a sustained harassment campaign (ibid.).
- Theft Act 1968 (Section 21): Used in cases where stolen images were exploited for blackmail (UK Government, 1968).
- Computer Misuse Act 1990: Relevant when images were obtained through hacking or unauthorized access (UK Government, 1990).
- Obscene Publications Act 1959: Rarely applicable, as intimate images would typically not meet the legal definition of obscene[6] (UK Government, 1959).

However, these laws were inadequate, forcing courts to interpret pre-Internet statutes in ways that did not fully address the harm caused by digital abuse. Certainly, the early experience of the Professionals Online Safety highlighted that laws could not be consistently applied, and the criminal justice system would, it would sometimes seem, go out of its way to find reasons why these pieces of pre-Internet legislation could not be applied in these cases. Therefore, victims were left (as we can see

[6] In the UK, the legal threshold for obscenity is primarily determined by the Obscene Publications Act 1959 (OPA 1959) and other related laws. Under the OPA 1959, material is deemed obscene if "Its effect, taken as a whole, is such as to tend to deprave and corrupt persons who are likely, having regard to all relevant circumstances, to read, see, or hear the matter contained or embodied in it". This means that if material has the potential to morally corrupt or degrade those who are likely to encounter it, it may be considered obscene under UK law.

above) at the mercy of individuals in the justice system to accept these laws could be applied or make use of civil claims to gain any form of resource. It seemed very clear that, due to the specific online nature of the acts, and the significant impact upon victim's well-being, that new legislation was necessary to remove this web of legislative and prosecutorial decision making on individual cases. If a law was defined specifically by the state that the non-consensual sharing of intimate images was a crime, it was hoped outcomes for victims would significantly improve.

During the parliamentary discussions on what became the Criminal Justice and Courts Act 2015, informed significantly by the Professionals Online Safety Helpline and the cases that they were encountering, MP Maria Miller, a politician who had been engaged with the work of the Helpline since prior to its inception, highlighted the impact on victims, particularly women, who suffered career damage and personal distress from revenge porn. Her advocacy led to the eventual creation of the new law.

Mrs Miller led the debate,[7] arguing that the existing legal framework had failed to keep pace with digital advancements, leaving victims—predominantly women—without sufficient protection. She emphasized that the act of sharing intimate images without consent was a form of sexual abuse, often resulting in severe emotional distress, career damage, and social isolation.

One of the key concerns raised was that search engines and social media platforms facilitated the spread of these images yet lacked legal obligations to remove them. Websites hosting revenge pornography operated freely, sometimes even charging victims to have their images removed. This had, again, been something that the helpline had encountered when trying to get images taken down on behalf of victims and something we will return to in discussing technical interventions as an issue such as NCII presents some challenges in this context.

The legal gaps were a major focus of the debate. Although it was acknowledged that some existing laws—such as the Protection from Harassment Act 1997 and the Communications Act 2003—could be

[7] https://hansard.parliament.uk/Commons/2014-06-19/debates/14061947000003/RevengePornography.

applied in certain cases, they were not designed to address the unique nature of revenge pornography. Victims often struggled to get law enforcement to act, as police officers lacked the necessary training and awareness (something that, we can evidence, remains the case). Additionally, prosecutions were rare because the legal framework required evidence of intent to cause distress, making convictions difficult.

The Government response, represented by Justice Minister Shailesh Vara, acknowledged these concerns and agreed that the law needed to be strengthened. While existing laws provided some protection, they did not directly criminalize the non-consensual sharing of intimate images. The debate ultimately contributed to the introduction of specific IIA laws in the Criminal Justice and Courts Act 2015 (specifically Section 33) (ibid.), making it an offence to disclose private sexual images without consent.

Section 33 Criminal Justice and Courts Act 2015

Ultimately, these debates resulted in the assent of the Criminal Justice and Courts Act 2015 with Section 33 of the legislation specifically referred to as the first revenge pornography legislation in England and Wales. This law makes it a criminal offence to disclose private sexual photographs or films without consent, provided the perpetrator intended to cause distress to the individual depicted.

Under Section 33, an individual commits an offence if they:

1. Disclose a private sexual photograph or film of another person.
2. Do so without the consent of the person depicted.
3. Do so with the intention of causing distress.

The offence covers a wide range of disclosure methods, including:

- Posting images on social media platforms.
- Sharing via messaging apps like WhatsApp, Snapchat, or Telegram.
- Sending explicit content through email or text messages.

- Uploading images or videos to pornographic websites.
- Distributing printed or digital copies via physical means.

And to qualify as "private and sexual", the content must depict:

- A person engaging in sexual activity.
- Exposed genitals, buttocks, or breasts.
- Material that a reasonable person would consider sexually explicit.

And there are limited defences in the legislation available to those accused of revenge pornography. The law allows for exceptions in cases where:

- The accused reasonably believed they had consent to share the material.
- The disclosure was for the purposes of journalism or law enforcement.
- The image had previously been made public with the full consent of the person depicted.

Section 33 Issues—Reflections from the Helpline

While the legislation was undoubtedly progress in supporting victims of IIA, it soon became clear that having a law to specifically address a harm does not immediately rectify the issues faced by victims. Over the next few years, Helpline cases highlighted both flaws in the legislation, and also where the broader ecosystem, something we return to in later chapters, also needs to engage with the issues.

Intention to Cause Distress

The 2015 legislation included an intention to cause distress requirement: in the stereotypical scenario that the law was designed to tackle, the perpetrator was assumed to have exactly that intention. However, the unintended consequence was that offenders could avoid legal repercussions for their actions by claiming some *other* intention: that they shared images for laugh, that they didn't think the victim would mind, even that they had shared the images for financial gain. The law specifically excluded the fact that it was a foreseeable consequence that a victim might be caused distress, only the intention of the perpetrator mattered. The effect on the victim simply didn't matter at all.

Some jurisdictions retain this intention requirement, and disappointingly, Article 16 of the upcoming UN Cybercrime Convention (United Nations, 2024), that will make it a requirement for all member states to have legislation on the sharing of intimate images without consent, states that "A State Party may require the intent to cause harm before criminal liability attaches". The UK has learned from experience that the intention criterion leaves too many gaps that offenders can move through to evade justice. And basing an offence on the motivations of the perpetrator strip the victim of their bodily autonomy just as surely as the offence itself. The only acceptable approach must be one of consent: private, sexual images of a person may only be shared on the basis that the person or people depicted have given their consent.

Threats to Share

The 2015 legislation did not originally include *threats* to share intimate images but this is something that we see regularly on the Helpline. Often a former partner will make threats to share intimate images to try to coerce the victim back into a relationship with them or to punish them for ending a relationship. Current partners can also use these threats to stop the victim leaving the relationship. In 2018, a woman came to the Helpline after 18 months of continuous threats from a former partner that he would share nude images and videos of her that he had taken when they were together; he said he would upload them to an adult site in her new partner's name with her contact details and full name. He also told her he would send them specifically to her new partner, to her mother, sister and friends, and that he would share them to her workplace. The victim was terrified and came to us for help because she was entirely drained and exhausted. She eventually reported what was happening to the police and they investigated it as a case of harassment.

In 2020, Refuge launched a campaign called "The Naked Threat"[8] which revealed research on the prevalence of threats to share intimate images without consent. The research found that 1 in 14 adults in England and Wales had experienced such threats, equivalent to 4.4 million. At the same time, Refuge demanded that the Government use the then Domestic Abuse Bill to make such threats illegal, and they did. In 2021, the Domestic Abuse Act (UK Government, 2021) added threats to the original sharing offence.

"Deepfakes"

Another specific exclusion from the 2015 Act were images that had been altered or manipulated in order to show an intimate image of someone. Most commonly now this would be what we refer to as "deepfakes", or synthetic sexual content, but at the time was more usually reported to the Helpline as images created with Photoshop. It was felt that, although such images would be distressing, "we do not believe that they have the potential to cause as much harm as disclosure of photographs and films that record real sexual private events".[9] Perhaps it was thought that such technologies would remain niche and require more skill than the average person was likely to have, but that has proved not to be the case in the years since. The advent of AI generative technologies in this area has led to an explosion of ways in which ordinary pictures of women can be stripped to make the woman appear nude.

In 2019, a developer known only as "Alberto", launched an app called DeepNude which could take a single image of a clothed woman and make it nude (Gockel, 2024). Almost immediately, demand for the app was overwhelming and the servers crashed it so that within days, Alberto decided to take the site down all together. He claimed to be surprised himself with the demand that appeared overnight, having expected only to sell the software occasionally. Since then, the number of apps and sites

---

[8] https://refuge.org.uk/news/refuge-launches-the-naked-threat-campaign/.

[9] Hansard (HL), 20 October 2014, vol 765, col 525.

that allow users to create AI-generated nude images, "nudify" or "face swap" has increased exponentially (Maras & Logie, 2024). And they have become much easier to use: what used to require some technical skill can now be created in seconds with easy-to-use software and only needing a single original image. A woman who came to the Helpline in 2020 was a teacher who had had synthetic sexual images created of her and shared online on Instagram and Twitter from where they were shared to her school community. The teacher ended up being sacked by the school for gross misconduct because they said the images were genuinely of her and that she must have uploaded them herself. At no time was she given any support or treated as a victim of any crime. She was devastated by the loss of her career and described herself as "utterly disappointed, angry and upset".

Women are disproportionately affected by this form of abuse. Most of these technologies only work on women and women are predominantly the sex targeted. Research from Security Hero (2023) found that 98% of the deepfakes online were pornographic and, of those, 99% of the individuals targeted were women. In 2024, when the legislation around the sharing of intimate images without consent was replaced, the new definition of an image included fake or synthetic images and they would be treated in exactly the same way as genuine images. Work is continuing to criminalize the creation of such images, which is discussed further in Chapter 5.

Definition of an Intimate Image (England and Wales)

The original definition of an intimate image was narrowly defined in the 2015 legislation. An image had to be both "private" and "sexual": the definition of "private" was straightforward ("something that is not of a kind ordinarily seen in public") but sexual required that:

> "(a) it shows all or part of an individual's exposed genitals or pubic area,
> (b) it shows something that a reasonable person would consider to be sexual because of its nature, or
> (c) its content, taken as a whole, is such that a reasonable person would consider it to be sexual".

This definition excluded large numbers of images that, if shared without consent of the person in them, would cause huge harm. The drafting shows a lack of understanding of the types of images that people share and the devastation that can be caused by their abuse. For example, an image of a woman in underwear would not have fallen within the definition, perhaps the assumption was that there would be no difference between that image and a woman in a bikini. The Helpline has been reporting images for one woman for some years now who has a number of images of her in underwear that have been widely shared: readers will have to take my word for it, but the context of these images, and what they show, is a long way from a bikini image and the devastation that has been caused by their sharing on the woman depicted has been far-reaching and long-lasting.

This definition also excluded images that more conservative communities and cultures might consider intimate but would not fall within the understanding of "private sexual". This is explored further in Chapter 5, but it is important to remember that definitions of intimacy vary, not just globally, but within the UK or any other country. It is important that, when considering violations such as intimate image abuse, we are sensitive to variations in what is considered acceptable.

As noted above, this definition also specifically excluded images that had been altered and/or combined in such a way that "it is only private or sexual by virtue of the alteration or combination",[10] which at the time were largely images created or altered by Photoshop, but now we would think of as AI generated or "deepfake".

Anonymity

The final major area of concern with the 2015 legislation concerned anonymity for victims, or rather, the lack of it. The original crime was classified as a communications offence which meant there was no guarantee of anonymity for victims. For someone whose privacy, bodily and sexual autonomy have been so traumatically stripped away, the prospect

---

[10] Criminal Justice and Courts Act 2015, s33(5)(b) [*repealed*].

of attending a public courtroom with no protection was unthinkable. Most clients who come to the Helpline do not report to the police; they simply want their images removed from the internet. And we know through Freedom of Information requests that, of the cases designated No Further Action, a third of those are because the victim withdraws their support. Repeatedly, women say to us "I want to contact the police, but I don't want to go to court", "I do not want to cause myself further distress by for example going to court" and "I really don't want it to be escalated and go to court". This is often because it raises the likelihood of more people finding out what has happened, in particular, family members, partners and workplaces and all the further consequences of that: damaged personal relationships, job progression and career prospects and the impacts on psychological and emotional well-being. Most people that come to the Helpline want the immediate issue resolved promptly and then forget that such a terrible thing ever happened. They do not want to go through the additional trauma and revictimization of going through the criminal justice system.

Responses by Other Nations in the UK

In 2016, the Government in Scotland passed the Abusive Behaviour and Sexual Harm Act (UK Government, 2016) to make it a criminal offence to share intimate images without consent, similar to the law that had been passed the previous year covering England and Wales. There were, however, some crucial differences in the Scottish legislation.

Firstly, the law created an offence of *threatening* to share at the same time as one of *sharing* images (s 2). Secondly, the definition of an intimate image includes photographs or films that show "the person's genitals, buttocks or breasts are exposed or covered only with underwear" (s 3(1)(b)) and finally, the images themselves, both photographs and film, can be "in any form, whether or not the image has been altered in any way" thus including synthetic or "deepfake", or Photoshopped, images. This divergence from the approach taken in England and Wales felt significant and progressive, capturing a broader range of potential offences than their counterparts in England and Wales, who were attempting to capture a narrower range of abuses.

At a similar time, in Northern Ireland, the Justice Act (Northern Ireland) 2016 (Northern Ireland Assembly, 2016) created offences of sharing intimate images without consent for that part of the UK. They were drafted to reflect the 2015 legislation that was in force at the time in England and Wales that has now been superseded and therefore raise many of the concerns outlined above: the lack of anonymity, the definition of an intimate image and the inclusion of an intention to cause distress. In 2022, threats to share intimate images were included in the 2016 Act.

The legislative landscape of this issue is a complex one in the UK: four nations originally had two different sets of legislation and now have three, with differing definitions, intentions and protections for victims. Such complications are extremely difficult for victims to understand in times of crisis and present multiple challenges to the Helpline. People are often reluctant to share personal information so there is a risk that we give incorrect information simply because we don't know exactly where someone is. While I have repeatedly called for consistency globally in the approach to the law in this area, establishing a consistent context across the single country of the UK would be a very good start.

Addressing Gaps in the Law

Nevertheless, it is to the credit of the policy space that there was acknowledgement of these issues emerging both from the academic literature (for example, Phippen and Brennan [2020] and McGlynn et al. [2017]) and considerable lobbying effort by the Helpline.

In 2021 a major review of IIA was conducted by the Law Commission (2021). The Law Commission is the independent statutory body in England and Wales responsible for reviewing, updating, and reforming the law. This review was something with which all the authors involved in this book were heavily involved. The review engaged with a broad range of stakeholders who voiced consistent concerns around issues such as threat and intention to harm. In producing a final report on the consultation, they focused on several key issues that reflected both Helpline experiences:

- Public vs. Private Images: The legal distinction between images taken in public vs. private spaces remains ambiguous. Some consultees were concerned about how courts would determine whether an image was taken in a public or private setting.
- Possession and Retention of Images: There was debate about whether simply possessing or retaining an intimate image without consent should be criminalized, particularly when there is a request to delete the image.
- Children and Young People: There were concerns that criminalizing minors for intimate image abuse could lead to overcriminalization and fail to address the issue through education and rehabilitation rather than punishment.
- Altered and Fake Images: The report discusses the rise of deepfake technology and "nudified" images, and whether such digitally manipulated images should fall within the scope of intimate image abuse offences.

And several recommendations were made including:

- The introduction of new offences:
- Criminalizing the taking or sharing of intimate images without consent.
- Specific offences for images shared with intent to humiliate, alarm, or distress the victim.
- Criminalizing threats to share intimate images, regardless of whether the images exist.
- Enhancing Sentencing Guidelines: Calls for harsher penalties, with proposed maximum sentences of two to three years for offences with aggravating factors.
- Automatic Anonymity for Victims: Like sexual offence victims, victims of intimate image abuse should have their identities automatically protected in legal proceedings.

- Review of Prosecutorial Guidelines: The Crown Prosecution Service (CPS) is recommended to update guidance on intimate image abuse, particularly regarding cases involving children.

As can be seen, many these recommendations are in line with the issues the Helpline had identified in the years after the 2015 legislation and these observations strongly informed the review.

The review also acknowledged several broader societal issues that would require further legislative development:

- Impact on Women and Girls: The report acknowledges that intimate image abuse is often gendered, disproportionately affecting women and girls, and highlights its links to misogyny and online abuse.
- Role of Social Media Platforms: Discussion on platform liability, with recommendations for stronger regulations to prevent intimate image abuse on digital platforms.
- Education and Awareness: A strong call for better education on intimate image abuse in schools, including teaching young people about consent and digital safety.

During the Law Commission review there was development of a new broad piece of legislation around Domestic Abuse, which became the Domestic Abuse Act 2021 (UK Government, 2021). This new legislation enabled the swift implementation of one of the recommendations of the Law Commission review which, in turn, had been driven by calls from stakeholders, such as us, in the IIA ecosystem. This new criminal offence centred on threatening to disclose intimate images.

With the passage of the Domestic Abuse Act 2021, specifically Section 69 (Bettinson et al., 2023), it was now an offence to:

- Threaten to share private sexual images or videos, even if the images are never actually disclosed.
- Make such threats without the consent of the individual depicted.
- Use threats as a means of coercion or emotional abuse.

Furthermore, in the offence of threat to share, there was no requirement for proof that the perpetrator intended to cause distress—the very act of making the threat is enough to constitute a crime.

In further legislative developments, the ubiquitous Online Safety Act 2023 (UK Government, 2023), which encompasses legislation more broadly than IIA also had a role to play in filling some of these gaps identified by our research and lobbying by the Helpline. A piece of legislation whose focus was significantly on the responsibilities of platforms to ensure that their users were able to engage in online activities in a safe manner, the Act assigned Ofcom[11] as the regulator, giving it the power to hold social media companies accountable for removing illegal content, protecting children from harmful material, and implementing age verification. It also introduces strict penalties for non-compliance, including heavy fines and potential criminal liability for tech executives. Nevertheless, it was also an opportunity to include stronger legislation around IIA, and address some of the concerns of the ecosystem.

Under the UK's Online Safety Act 2023, a priority offence refers to specific illegal activities that online platforms are required to proactively prevent and swiftly remove from their services. These offences are identified as particularly serious and prevalent, necessitating stringent measures to protect users from associated harms.

The Act categorizes priority offences into several key areas, including:

- Terrorism: Offences related to promoting or facilitating terrorist activities.
- Child Sexual Abuse and Exploitation: Crimes involving the abuse or exploitation of minors.
- Hate Crimes: Offences that incite violence or hatred against individuals or groups based on characteristics such as race, religion, or sexual orientation.
- Fraud and Financial Crimes: Activities involving deception for financial gain.

---

[11] Ofcom is the UK's communications regulator, overseeing online, TV, radio, telecoms, postal services, and wireless communications to ensure they operate fairly and within the law. https://www.ofcom.org.uk. Accessed May 2025.

- Drug and Weapon Offences: The sale or distribution of illegal drugs and weapons.
- Public Order Offences: Crimes that disturb public peace, including harassment and stalking.
- **Intimate Image Abuse: The non-consensual sharing of private sexual images, commonly known as "revenge porn".**

Through the legislation online platforms are mandated to assess the risks associated with these priority offences and implement effective systems and processes to mitigate and manage these risks. Failure to comply with these duties can result in enforcement actions by the regulatory authority, Ofcom, including substantial fines or other penalties.

Further enhancements of the legislation around IIA included:

- The Act introduces a broader set of offences related to the sharing, taking, or threatening to share intimate images without consent.
- It covers deepfake pornography, where AI-generated images or videos depict a person in an explicit way without their consent.
- Includes downblousing, which involves taking intrusive images down a person's top without consent.

Cyberflashing as a Criminal Offence:

- The Online Safety Act 2023 introduced a new specific offence of cyberflashing, making it illegal to send unsolicited sexual images without consent.
- The law applies to images sent electronically, covering social media, messaging apps, and proximity-based sharing methods like AirDrop.
- Key Legal Standard: The offence applies where the sender intended to cause alarm, distress, or humiliation OR acted for sexual gratification without reasonable belief in consent.

And the removal of the "Intent to Cause Distress" Requirement:

- Previously, under the Criminal Justice and Courts Act 2015, prosecutors had to prove the intent to cause distress when convicting someone for sharing revenge pornography.
- The Online Safety Act removes this requirement, making it easier to prosecute offenders who share intimate images for any reason without consent.

The Act introduces harsher sentences, including up to six months' imprisonment for sharing intimate images without consent and up to two years' imprisonment for more serious offences. It also prioritizes victim protection by allowing quicker removal of images from online platforms and aligns with other laws on domestic abuse and coercive control, recognizing that image-based abuse often occurs in abusive relationships. This is a significant step forward from original discussions that view IIA as a communications crime (Phippen & Brennan, 2020).

As is typical with the evolving nature of legislation in this area, the Online Safety Act 2023 arguably marks a significant step forward in addressing intimate image abuse by closing legislative gaps and providing stronger protections for victims. It certainly incorporated a lot of the recommendations from the Law Commission review on IIA. By expanding the scope of offences, removing barriers to prosecution, and introducing harsher penalties, the Act acknowledges the evolving nature of online abuse and the profound harm it can cause. Its provisions on cyberflashing, deepfake pornography, and downblousing demonstrate a commitment to tackling new forms of digital exploitation, while the emphasis on victim protection and platform accountability ensures that online spaces become safer.

Conclusions

Over the past decade, the legal framework surrounding intimate image abuse (IIA) in the UK has evolved significantly, moving from fragmented, pre-digital statutes to a more cohesive and targeted legislative response. The initial introduction of specific criminal offences in the *Criminal Justice and Courts Act 2015* marked a turning point, but also revealed critical gaps—particularly its narrow focus on perpetrator intent and limited definitions of what constitutes a "private" or "sexual" image.

A consistent theme throughout this chapter has been the role of real-world cases and victim experiences in pushing the law to evolve. In this context, the Revenge Porn Helpline has been one of the most influential actors in the UK's response to intimate image abuse. Since its establishment in 2015, just before the original legislation came into force, the Helpline has not only supported tens of thousands of victims but has also played a central role in documenting systemic shortcomings, advising policymakers, and contributing directly to legal reform.

Data gathered through Helpline cases provided some of the earliest and most sustained empirical evidence of where the 2015 law fell short—particularly around coercive threats, synthetic imagery (deepfakes), and the absence of victim anonymity. The Helpline's casework and frontline experience were cited in multiple government consultations, including the *Law Commission's 2021 review*, and informed major legislative updates such as the introduction of threats to share as a criminal offence in the *Domestic Abuse Act 2021*, and the removal of the intent requirement in the *Online Safety Act 2023*. In these areas, the Helpline's insights were not just advisory—they were foundational.

The Helpline also helped reframe public and political understanding of intimate image abuse as a form of gender-based violence and digital exploitation, rather than a niche or voyeuristic offence. It has highlighted the reality that victims often do not want to pursue criminal prosecution, but simply want the content removed and their privacy restored—insights that have informed platform accountability measures and helped shape a more victim-centred approach to the issue.

Legislative responses across the UK's four nations have differed in scope and pace, with Scotland and Northern Ireland at times implementing broader protections earlier. However, a recurring barrier across jurisdictions has been the complexity and inconsistency in legal definitions and protections—something that frontline organisations like the Helpline have continually had to navigate when supporting victims. Their calls for greater consistency, clarity, and equity in legal standards remain as relevant today as they were when the first "revenge porn" cases emerged.

What emerges from this chapter is a picture of gradual, hard-won progress driven by the intersection of victim advocacy, academic critique, legal analysis, and frontline experience. The evolution of the UK's legal framework has increasingly aligned with the realities of digital harm but this alignment has not occurred in a vacuum. It has been shaped and informed by those working directly with victims, none more so than the Revenge Porn Helpline, whose influence can be seen across every major legislative milestone discussed in this chapter.

References

Agate, J., & Ledward, J. (2013). Social media: How the net is closing in on cyber bullies. *Entertainment Law Review, 24*(8), 263–268.

Bettinson, V., Phippen, A., & Bond, E. (2023). Offences involving abuse of violent behaviour (Sections 68–69). In S. Edwards, D. Malone, & G. Jones (Eds.), *Blackstone's guide to the Domestic Abuse Act 2021.* Oxford University Press.

Brimblecombe, F., & Fenwick, H. (2022). Keeping control of personal information in the digital age: Efficacy and equivalence of tortious and GDPR/DPA remedial relief? *The Law Quarterly Review, 138,* 456–480. https://www.sweetandmaxwell.co.uk/en-gb/products/the-law-quarterly-review-journal-and-ejournal-subscription-30928223

Bustamante, D. (2016). Florida joins the fight against revenge porn: Analysis of Florida's new anti-revenge porn law. *FIU Law Review, 12,* 357.

Castle, C. (2021). *The duchess who dared: The life of Margaret, duchess of Argyll (The extraordinary story behind A Very British Scandal, starring Claire Foy and Paul Bettany).* Swift Press.

Dickie, H. J. (1966). Restraint of breach of confidence: Duchess of Argyll v. Duke of Argyll. *Faculty of Law Review, 24,* 115.

Gockel, J. (2024). The current state of pornographic deepfakes: A science and technology studies perspective. *The Maastricht Journal of Liberal Arts, 15.*

Hughes, K. (2014). Publishing photographs without consent. *Journal of Media Law, 6*(2), 180–192.

Kipnis, L. (2013). (Male) desire and (female) disgust: Reading Hustler. In *Cultural studies* (pp. 373–391). Routledge.

Law Commission. (2021). *Taking, Making and Sharing Intimate Images Without Consent.* https://lawcom.gov.uk/project/taking-making-and-sharing-intimate-images-without-consent/. Accessed May 2025.

Lintern-Davies, T., & Doherty, M. (2006). The role of conditional fee arrangements in relation to freedom of expression: Campbell v. MGN Limited [2005] UKHL 61. *The Law Teacher, 40*, 91.

Maras, M. H., & Logie, K. (2024). Countering the complex, multifaceted nature of nude and sexually explicit deepfakes: An Augean task? *Crime Science, 13*(1), 1–17.

McGlynn, C., Rackley, E., & Houghton, R. (2017). Beyond 'revenge porn': The continuum of image-based sexual abuse. *Feminist Legal Studies, 25*, 25–46.

Northern Ireland Assembly. (2016). *Justice Act (Northern Ireland) 2016*. https://www.legislation.gov.uk/nia/2016/21. Accessed May 2025.

Phippen, A., & Brennan, M. (2020). *Sexting and revenge pornography: Legislative and social dimensions of a modern digital phenomenon.* Routledge.

Pollack, J. M. (2016). Getting even: Empowering victims of revenge porn with a civil cause of action. *Albany Law Review, 80*, 353.

Security Hero. (2023). *State of Deepfakes.* https://www.securityhero.io/state-of-deepfakes/. Accessed May 2025.

UK Government. (1959). *Obscene Publications Act 1959.* https://www.legislation.gov.uk/ukpga/Eliz2/7-8/66. Accessed May 2025.

UK Government. (1968). *Theft Act 1968: Section 21.* https://www.legislation.gov.uk/ukpga/1968/60/section/21. Accessed May 2025.

UK Government. (1988). *Malicious Communications Act 1988.* https://www.legislation.gov.uk/ukpga/1988/27. Accessed May 2025.

UK Government. (1990). *Computer Misuse Act 1990.* https://www.legislation.gov.uk/ukpga/1990/18. Accessed May 2025.

UK Government. (1997). *Protection from Harassment Act 1997*. https://www.legislation.gov.uk/ukpga/1997/40. Accessed May 2025.

UK Government. (2003). *Communications Act 2003.* https://www.legislation.gov.uk/ukpga/2003/21. Accessed May 2025.

UK Government. (2015). *Criminal Justice and Courts Act 2015, c. 2, § 33.* https://www.legislation.gov.uk/ukpga/2015/2/section/33. Accessed May 2025.

UK Government. (2016). *Abusive Behaviour and Sexual Harm Act (Scotland).* https://www.legislation.gov.uk/asp/2016/22/section/2. Accessed May 2025.

UK Government. (2021). *Domestic Abuse Act 2021: Section 69*. Legislation.gov.uk. https://www.legislation.gov.uk/ukpga/2021/17/section/69/enacted. Accessed May 2025.

UK Government. (2023). *Online Safety Act 2023*. https://www.legislation.gov.uk/ukpga/2023/50. Accessed May 2025.

United Nations. (2024). *United Nations Convention against Cybercrime: Strengthening international cooperation for combating certain crimes committed by means of information and communications technology systems and for the sharing of evidence in electronic form of serious crimes* (A/RES/79/243). https://documents.un.org/access.nsf/get?DS=A%2FRES%2F79%2F243&Lang=E. Accessed May 2025.

4

The Victim's Voice and the Efficacy of Legislation

Abstract This chapter explores the complex and often painful realities of victims of Intimate Image Abuse (IIA) in the UK, focusing on the disconnection between legislative progress and the lived experiences of those impacted. While laws such as the *Criminal Justice and Courts Act 2015*, *Domestic Abuse Act 2021*, and *Online Safety Act 2023* have expanded legal protections against image-based sexual abuse, analysis of helpline case data, police outcomes, and criminal justice statistics reveals that only a fraction of victims achieve justice. The chapter foregrounds victim narratives to highlight persistent barriers, including fear of re-traumatization, low prosecution rates, and police inaction. It critiques a justice system that often prioritizes legislative form over practical function and urges a shift towards a more holistic, victim-centred approach that incorporates education, mental health support, rapid content take-down mechanisms, and institutional reform. The Revenge Porn Helpline is recognized as a vital actor, shaping policy and providing essential support, while recent developments such as the *Women and Equalities Committee 2025* report underscore the urgent need for consistent enforcement, victim anonymity, and resourced civil remedies.

S. Mortimer et al., *Ten Years of the Revenge Porn Helpline*, Palgrave Studies in Victims and Victimology, https://doi.org/10.1007/978-3-032-00614-1_4

Keywords Victim · Centred justice · Image · Based Sexual Abuse (IBSA) · Police response · Criminal justice outcomes · Legal · Advocacy disconnect

Over the past decade, the legal and societal understanding of intimate image abuse (IIA)-often termed "revenge porn" in popular discourse-has undergone significant evolution. Legislative developments in the UK, beginning with the Criminal Justice and Courts Act 2015 (UK Government, 2015) and culminating (thus far) in the Online Safety Act 2023 (UK Government, 2023), have sought to define, criminalize, and deter a range of behaviours associated with the non-consensual creation and distribution of intimate images. These laws have been driven, in part, by growing public awareness, increased reporting, and the tireless advocacy of victims who have spoken out despite enormous personal cost.

Yet the lived experiences of those targeted by this abuse often reveal a disheartening disconnection between law and justice. While legislation provides a critical framework for recognizing and penalizing image-based abuse, many victims still struggle to access meaningful remedies. For some, justice comes too late, or not at all. For others, the trauma of the legal process itself-marked by police inaction, procedural delays, or re-traumatization-becomes yet another layer of harm. This chapter seeks to centre those victim experiences, drawing on helpline case studies, legal milestones, and national data to explore not only how the law operates in theory, but how it functions in practice.

We begin with a series of landmark cases—high-profile and lesser-known—which illuminate both the devastating impact of IIA and the possibilities and limits of legal recourse. From Chrissy Chambers' landmark civil settlement to Georgia Harrison's vocal advocacy during a widely publicized criminal trial, these stories show how survivors have helped to shape public consciousness and legal reform. But they also expose the structural failings of the justice system, particularly for victims who are not public figures, or who lack the resources to pursue legal redress.

Drawing on empirical evidence, including Freedom of Information data and Ministry of Justice statistics, we then evaluate the effectiveness of current legislation. While prosecution and conviction rates have risen modestly, they remain strikingly low in comparison with the number of reports received. The data also points to troubling trends: victims withdrawing support for investigations, lack of evidence cited as a common reason for inaction, and widespread distrust in the criminal justice system.

This chapter also examines how victims describe their experiences, revealing patterns of language that express fear, shame, confusion, and a desperate desire for control and recognition. These accounts underscore a key argument of this chapter: legislation alone cannot address the profound personal and psychological impact of this crime. What victims require is not only justice in the traditional sense, but validation, protection, and support-none of which can be delivered by legal frameworks in isolation.

By centring the victim's voice and confronting the systemic shortcomings exposed by Helpline data, legal outcomes, and survivor narratives, this chapter argues for a more holistic approach to tackling intimate image abuse one that integrates legislation with institutional reform, education, and resourced victim support.

Case Milestones

Chrissy Chambers

In 2009, an eighteen year old American woman, living in Atlanta, Georgia, called Chrissy Chambers, was dating a British man she had met online. After nine months together she felt he was controlling within the relationship, so she told him she wanted to take a break. He suggested that they have a last night together, drinking alcohol. Chrissy, who had never been a drinker, ultimately blacked out, with no recollection of the night before waking up the next morning. That day, after a tearful goodbye, he left to go back to the UK and Chrissy Chambers got on with her life.

Four years later, in June 2013, Chrissy had come out as gay and, with her partner Bria, was running a successful YouTube channel of music, comedy, and support for LGBTQ+ rights. But then Chrissy received a message from a friend about a message that she had received about Chrissy that ended: "Just Google 'Chrissy Chambers porn'". Chrissy did and discovered a video of herself that she had never seen before and didn't know existed. It had been recorded in her old apartment, that last night with her ex-partner, and the film showed him having sex with her, impassive and unresponsive. In the following weeks, she discovered more videos that had spread to multiple adult sites. Her ex-partner had filmed himself having sex with her, without her knowledge or consent and, as she had been moving on with her life oblivious, he had been uploading the videos online. The video had already been online for 18 months before Chrissy even knew about it (Véliz, 2019).

In the weeks that followed, Chrissy and Bria worked hard to try and get the video removed from the online platforms, with limited success. They reported Chrissy's ex to the police in Atlanta, but they told her that even though the videos had been created in the USA, they had been uploaded in the UK so that was where she had to go. Months of toing and froing between the two countries, speaking to the police, searching for a lawyer and continually trying to remove the online videos took its toll but eventually Chrissy's case was taken on by Ann Olivarius, an American feminist lawyer whose firm was based in the UK. Olivarius had a long track record in sexual harassment and discrimination cases and, while managing Chrissy's expectations, she saw her case as an opportunity to change the legal framework of these cases in England and Wales. After extensive lobbying by lawyers, charities, campaign groups and victims/survivors, it became a criminal offence in April 2015 to share intimate images of someone without their consent with the intention to cause distress.

The new legislation was too late for Chrissy Chambers because her images had been shared in 2011, however, she made a complaint to the police in the hopes of a harassment charge, but this did not proceed due to a lack of evidence. But Chambers wasn't quitting and went public with a film about her ordeal, made with *The Guardian*[1] and she became an

[1] https://www.theguardian.com/uk-news/2015/jun/03/us-woman-pursues-ex-boyfriend-in-landmark-uk-revenge-porn-action. Accessed May 2025.

active and vocal campaigner on the issue of "revenge porn" in both the UK and the USA, all the while working with Olivarius and her firm to put together a civil case for damages. After a four-year long battle to get into court, out of the blue, her ex's lawyers got in touch and agreed to settle at the last minute. Significantly, as well as an apology and substantial financial damages, Chambers was also awarded the copyright for the images, empowering her to pursue takedowns from the sites sharing her images. Chambers' hard-won victory broke new ground, paving the way for new criminal law and a demonstration that victory could also be found in civil courts. *The Guardian* reported,[2] "Having broken new legal ground once again, Olivarius is delighted. She told us Chambers' victory would set a landmark precedent for other revenge-porn victims to follow, paving the way for other victims of revenge porn to sue for damages. With both a civil and a criminal path to justice, it has become less likely that those who post revenge porn will get away with it".

Chrissy Chambers' fight for justice was well-covered in the media, as was her ultimate victory. Despite the fact that the criminal law in the UK came too late to help her, the timing of her case and her use of her online platform to campaign on the issue, not to mention her courage in speaking out so publicly, mean she is the first high-profile case of this abuse that really cut through. While the media have covered these cases consistently since 2015, if anything, the tone has become more sensationalist. While I'm thankful that coverage of Chambers was predominantly respectful, that isn't always the case.

Zara McDermott

Zara McDermott, at age 21, appeared on the TV reality series *Love Island* in 2018. Contestants on the show, while on the island, don't have their phones so they don't know what is being said about them in the outside world. But when she left the show, the TV production team had to tell her that while she had been there, intimate images of her had been shared publicly, allegedly by a former partner, and the story was being covered

[2] https://www.theguardian.com/news/2018/jan/18/chrissy-chambers-youtube-revenge-porn-legal-victory. Accessed May 2025.

in the media. This was devastating, understandably, Zara described it, "I can't even tell you the feeling, feeling like your parents are ashamed of you... How will they look at me the same ever again? It was so embarrassing. I just wanted to die".

Now, in 2025, Zara's career has moved into television, presenting and producing documentaries. Yet almost every media article about her mentions her "revenge porn" experience, whether it's relevant or not. In 2021, Zara produced a documentary[3] called *Revenge Porn* (Skočir, 2024) where she talked about her own experiences of the issue, spoke to her family and partner about what had happened and also to other girls and young women affected. It was a courageous act, to discuss such private things so openly, and the expression of the impact on her will have resonated with many. But the documentary also raised concerns about how this issue is reported and reinforced a culture that says the victim is to blame for what happens to them.

One factor that is particularly disturbing, and that is often mentioned, including by Zara herself, is that she has been a victim of revenge porn *twice*.[4] This is referring to the fact that, when Zara was 14 years old, she was persuaded by a boy at school to send him intimate images of herself which he then shared around the school, leading to her being suspended while he faced no consequences. Putting aside the problematic nature of the phrase "revenge porn", what happened to Zara when she was 14 was in no way the same as what happened when she was 21. At 14, those images of Zara were child sexual abuse material and the sharing of them, even by another minor, was a serious criminal offence. The assumption was made that the sharing of the images was a sexual act on her part, when in reality it was about low self-esteem, a need for approval and simply wanting to be liked. She was failed by those around her then and when she had images shared of her in 2021, she was failed again by all those asking her how she could make the "same mistake" and should have been "more wise to it". It is disappointing to see such narratives aired

[3] https://www.bbc.co.uk/bbcthree/article/b80a18ed-e1e9-4fc5-9400-afba5f736c9d. Accessed May 2025.

[4] https://news.sky.com/story/love-island-star-zara-mcdermott-backs-online-safety-bill-to-stop-abuse-and-cyberbullying-12350850. Accessed May 2025.

without challenge and victims continue to be blamed while perpetrators escape the consequences.

"Victoria"[5]

In 2017, an anonymous woman referred to as "Victoria", found intimate images of her that had been taken without her knowledge or consent on her partner's laptop while he was away. There were photos of her sleeping naked, in the shower and cleaning alongside indecent images of children. She reported it all to the police who subsequently found hidden cameras as well as more voyeuristic content of Victoria and other women. In 2020, her ex-partner, Stuart Gaunt, was convicted of three counts of voyeurism and two counts of making an indecent image of a child, receiving a two year suspended prison sentence. But Victoria knew that, in the years since she had discovered that the images were online, they would only have spread further and further. Despite her criminal conviction, nothing would be done about the images circulating online. So, she took a case against him to the High Court (Welsh, 2025).

In February 2023, Victoria was awarded £60,000 in damages, which had taken into account psychiatric injury and the violation of her personal dignity. She was also awarded financial losses of £37,000 which included £21,600 to pay for a specialist company to remove the images from the internet. For Victoria, the case was a "triumph" and she was "thrilled" that other women might benefit from her action, but she knew that "[s]adly it won't ever be over. The fear is constantly there, that there is material stored somewhere that I don't know about". And this is the reality for survivors like Victoria: the images had circulated so widely, and it took so long for this judgement to come, that it is impossible to guarantee that these images will never surface again. The court ordered a private reputation management company to remove the pictures and videos of Victoria from the internet, but even they acknowledged the difficulties: "Someone will post something on a mainstream site and

[5] https://www.thetimes.com/uk/law/article/my-ex-posted-naked-photos-of-me-i-was-awarded100-000-to-wipe-them-90hn7577d. Accessed May 2025.

then smaller websites will copy the video and upload it themselves", said Niki Mistry, who works for the company. "So that one link very quickly becomes 50″. If the victim owns the content, then the company can use copyright laws to request the websites take it down. If they do not—like Victoria—they use criminal court documents, proving voyeurism or image-based sexual abuse. If they have neither, then the company simply has to ask the sites to remove it. They often refuse. The process generally takes six months".[6] I have no doubt this company has done its best for Victoria, however, the services of companies like these are beyond the financial reach of many. The Revenge Porn Helpline will support victims with content removal for free and their preventative tool, StopNCII.org is free to use for all adults globally.

Georgia Harrison

The most high-profile case, and most high-profile survivor of this abuse in recent years, is Georgia Harrison. Georgia was a contestant on *Love Island* and had appeared on *The Only Way is Essex*. For a while she dated another reality contestant called Stephen Bear (SB) and after they split up, they remained friends. In August 2020, they spent the afternoon together and had sex in his garden. Unbeknownst to Georgia, SB had CCTV cameras in his garden which had recorded the whole encounter. Later than evening, SB casually mentioned the CCTV; Georgia was horrified and made it clear that she did not give permission for that video to exist or be shared and asked him to delete it, which SB said he did. But that October, Georgia discovered that, not only had SB *not* deleted the video, but that he had uploaded it to his OnlyFans account and from there, it had spread across multiple adult sites. She reported what had happened to the police and he was arrested in January 2021 and later charged with one count of voyeurism and two counts of sharing intimate images without consent. General delays in the criminal justice system, exacerbated by the COVID-19 pandemic, meant that the case didn't come to trial until late 2022. Not surprisingly, the trial was conducted in

---

[6] https://www.thetimes.com/uk/law/article/my-ex-posted-naked-photos-of-me-i-was-awarded100-000-to-wipe-them-90hn7577d. Accessed May 2025.

the media spotlight, with SB encouraging the attention by grandstanding outside in flashy suits and cars, while inside he was rude and disruptive to the proceedings. He was found guilty and in March 2023 was sentenced to 21 months in prison, of which ultimately, he served ten and a half months inside (West, 2024).

Georgia has spoken openly about the impact that the sharing of the video has had on her life.[7] She felt ashamed and humiliated, brands that had paid her backed away. She couldn't afford to stay in her flat and moved back in with her mum. But, despite the fact that the voyeurism charge that SB was facing, which as a sexual offence, guaranteed the victim anonymity, Georgia chose to waive that right and speak up. For many victims of this abuse it is a very difficult thing to tell anyone what has happened, and for some, it is frankly impossible. But Georgia Harrison spent the time between SB's charges and the trial, campaigning for changes in the law and better protections for victims. She advocated for changes that had been proposed by the Law Commission which the government then included in the Online Safety Act which passed in October 2023 (UK Government, 2023). Most importantly, she refused to accept the shame as hers to live with which in turn gave validation to other victims to believe that what had happened to them was not their fault.

Georgia has continued to stand up for the rights of women affected by this abuse, attending conferences and events, and speaking to the press, reliving her own experience and outlining the expectations of victims to mitigate the harms they are experiencing. She still receives multiple messages daily from women who have had similar experiences but may feel less able to speak up. In March 2024, Georgia featured in a documentary that described her experience and how she was affected. And in early 2025 she produced a second documentary, that went beyond her own experience to show how intimate content online continues to spread, digging into the underlying financial motives that drive the spread of this content. As part of the documentary, Georgia visited the Revenge Porn Helpline to find out just how far her intimate images had spread. The answer was uncomfortable, and she has had to become

[7] https://www.bbc.co.uk/news/articles/c3d53m0gd2do. Accessed May 2025.

resigned to the reality that these images will continue to exist online. She said, "I would say obviously the hardest part for me was having to see how widespread my video still is…It's always something in the back of my mind, but having to really face head on exactly where it is and how many places it's in was a real struggle for me". It is to her credit that she allows this to empower her to continue to fight for victims to have the legal right for these images to be removed.

Reporting to the Police and the Criminal Justice System

Clearly, the cases outlined above do not illustrate everyone's experience when faced with intimate image abuse. However, they provide important milestones in the evolution of our responses to this abuse over the last ten years. And cases such as these serve to bring the harms of this abuse into the national line of sight, the potential remedies through the police and courts and instil the message that the sharing of these images without consent is simply wrong. But these cases have only become well-known because of their success, which is not the reality for most victims.

When someone calls the Helpline for advice, we always recommend that they report what has happened to the police. But many victims are clear that they don't want to make a report, they simply want to get their images removed and then forget that this ever happened. One woman said that she "didn't want to go to the police and report this as I don't know the consequences. As well as this i want to keep this private" while another said "I don't necessarily want to go to the police, I just want the photos gone".

And many who go to the police report negative experiences. One man who experienced extensive abuse from his ex-wife said: "Myself and my partner reported this to the police and to be honest they didn't help at all. They lost the case details and then they took months to even attempt to do anything". One woman reported that her ex-partner had her old phone which contained multiple intimate images of her, threatened to share the images, printed them out and threatened to send them to her mother and shared them online and then removed them but when she reported to the police was told that no laws had been broken. It is very common that the police place all the expectation of investigation and location of evidence on the victim, one woman reporting "We did go to the police station but they're unwilling to help unless we find out who has done it".

Another barrier for women to report to the police is simply the process involved which requires victims to show their images, repeatedly to, frequently male, police officers, having devices taken, images stored and shared with prosecutors and defence and then shown in court. Often victims are told that they have to leave the images live online until the case goes to court, which can take months or even years. The process can be overwhelming and intimidating to contemplate, so it is no surprise that many victims simply don't want to go through with it.

Impact on Victims

Helpline case data provides a disturbing glimpse into the emotional and psychological impacts on victims of intimate image abuse, revealing a pattern of debilitating anxiety, shame, depression, and, in some cases, suicidal thoughts. The abuse is not simply a digital violation, it is a profound attack on a victim's sense of security, self-worth and personal autonomy.

For many victims, the overriding emotional response is fear. The mere threat of exposure can send them into a state of lasting panic, unsure of when or if their images will surface. This anxiety is compounded by shame and self-blame. Many victims turn their anger inward, questioning how they could have been so trusting, how they allowed themselves to be manipulated, or how they did not see the warning signs. A woman whose ex-boyfriend leaked her private images admitted that she stopped looking at herself in the mirror because she felt disgusted by her own body, as though she were responsible for what had happened to her. Logically, she knew she had done nothing wrong, but emotionally she could not separate her violation from her own sense of self-worth.

For male victims, the shame manifests differently. Many struggle with the fear of being seen as weak, worrying that if they speak out, they will be mocked rather than supported. One man, who was blackmailed after exchanging intimate messages online, described feeling completely alone and humiliated, unable to seek help because he was convinced that no one would take him seriously. Instead of reporting the crime, he withdrew into himself, becoming increasingly isolated and distrustful of others.

This loss of trust is a recurring emotional wound. Victims struggle not only with the betrayal of the person who exposed them but also with a deep, underlying fear that anyone they meet in the future might do the same. One woman, who discovered that her partner had secretly recorded their intimate moments, described how her ability to trust was shattered beyond repair. Even after breaking up with him, she found herself incapable of forming new relationships, constantly questioning the motives of anyone who showed interest in her.

For victims deceived by fake online identities and catfishing scams, the betrayal cuts just as deep. A man who was lured into sending explicit images to someone he thought was a romantic interest admitted that he could never bring himself to engage with dating apps again, fearing that every interaction was a trap waiting to happen. This hyper-vigilance and withdrawal from social interaction can lead to profound loneliness, as victims feel safer isolating themselves rather than risking further abuse.

As time goes on, the relentless stress and fear can lead victims into a state of emotional numbness. What begins as panic and desperation often deteriorates into depression and exhaustion. Some victims describe feeling as though their lives are permanently tainted, as if, no matter what they do, they will always be defined by this one event.

For those whose images continue to circulate online, the emotional damage is even greater. A woman whose photos were uploaded to adult websites without her consent described how she spent years filing takedown requests, only to find that new uploads kept appearing under different names. Eventually, she gave up, saying that she felt like she no longer existed as a person, only as an image on the internet, completely outside of her control.

Perhaps the most disturbing revelation in the case data is the prevalence of suicidal thoughts among victims. Many describe reaching a point where they feel there is no way out, believing that death is preferable to the humiliation and exposure they are facing. Sextortion cases, in particular, have an extremely high risk of suicidal ideation, as victims, especially young men, fear complete social and professional ruin. One young man who was being blackmailed reported to the Helpline that he had seriously considered ending his life, believing that his reputation was beyond repair.

Fortunately, many victims find support systems in family, friends, or support services, which help them begin the slow process of recovery. However, many report feeling completely alone, especially when the police fail to take their cases seriously or when websites do little to remove their images.

This abuse is a direct assault on a person's mental and emotional well-being. The emotional and psychological scars left behind are deep and lasting, affecting a victim's ability to trust, feel safe, and even function in daily life. For many, the worst part is not the initial violation, it is the endless cycle of fear, shame, and helplessness that follows, knowing that at any moment, their privacy could be violated all over again.

Without stronger legal protections, rapid content removal processes, and better victim support systems, intimate image abuse will continue to leave behind a trail of psychological devastation. Victims do not just need justice: they need acknowledgment, understanding, and a society that doesn't blame them for crimes committed against them.

The Language of Distress

The language used in intimate image abuse enquiries reveals a deep sense of distress, urgency, and helplessness. Victims do not approach these issues with the confidence of someone filing a standard complaint; rather, their words are often filled with panic, uncertainty, and a desperate plea for help. The way they phrase their enquiries reflects not just the violation they have endured, but also the emotional devastation it has caused and the level of self-blame they are feeling.

Most messages are deeply personal, with victims using direct and intimate language as they recount their experiences. They frequently refer to themselves, emphasizing the violation as something that has happened to them, rather than as a general issue. This makes sense: intimate image abuse is deeply invasive and personal, and those affected often struggle to separate the crime from their own sense of identity. Many express their fear and confusion through uncertain, searching language, trying to piece together what has happened to them, how their images were leaked, and whether there is any way to regain control.

There is often an underlying tone of desperation in the way victims ask for help. Many plead rather than demand, using words that suggest they do not expect immediate assistance but are instead hoping someone will listen. There is a sense that they are uncertain whether help is even possible, and their messages frequently read as though they are asking for guidance as much as intervention. Some victims seem to be writing not just to report what has happened, but to make sense of it themselves, as if trying to process their violation in real-time.

A recurring theme in their language is a struggle to define the crime they have experienced. Victims often describe what happened in fragmented or hesitant terms, uncertain of the legal definitions but certain of the deep violation they feel. The word choices suggest that many are trying to find the right terminology to express their situation, particularly if they are unsure whether their case will be taken seriously.

For some, there is a strong focus on who did this to them. Many victims refer directly to the person responsible, particularly in cases where the perpetrator is an ex-partner, acquaintance, or someone they trusted. This suggests that many victims see justice as a key part of the solution, wanting not just content removal but accountability. Others, however, struggle with anonymity, particularly in cases of sextortion or online impersonation, where the abuser hides behind fake accounts and disposable emails. Their language reflects frustration and helplessness, as they describe trying to trace or understand who is behind the threats.

A significant proportion of messages carry a tone of fear and paranoia, particularly in cases where images have already been shared or where there is an ongoing threat of exposure. Victims frequently express a sense of impending doom, as though their entire life could be ruined at any moment. They ask where their images might be, who has seen them, and whether they can ever truly be erased. Their words often suggest relentless anxiety and an overwhelming sense of powerlessness.

The language used by victims also reveals a deep distrust in the systems meant to protect them. Many enquiries reference social media platforms, legal institutions, or helplines, often with a note of frustration or resignation. There is a sense that victims do not believe they will receive a timely or effective response, and in some cases, they seem exhausted before they have even begun the reporting process. Their words suggest that they have already been dismissed elsewhere, and they are now searching for someone who will take them seriously.

Ultimately, the way victims describe their experiences highlights the profound emotional impact of intimate image abuse. Their words do not read like a formal complaint but rather a cry for help, filled with fear, confusion, and a desperate need for reassurance. Many seem uncertain about whether justice is possible, but they reach out anyway, hoping that someone will listen.

Understanding Offender Behaviour in Image-Based Abuse Cases

This chapter is titled "The Victim's Voice" as we examine the experiences of, and consequences for, victims of intimate image abuse. Understanding this is key to developing effective strategies to give meaningful support; but alongside this we need to improve our understanding of perpetrator motivations if we hope to combat the underlying attitudes that drive this behaviour.

Helpline case data reveals distinct patterns in how offenders engage in intimate image abuse, highlighting their manipulative tactics, motivations and methods of coercion. These behaviours range from financial extortion and intimate image sharing to hacking and long-term harassment, often leaving victims feeling powerless and deeply traumatized.

One of the most prevalent forms of abuse observed in the dataset is sextortion, where perpetrators deceive victims, often posing as attractive individuals on social media or dating apps, into sharing intimate images. Once these images are obtained, the offender's approach shifts abruptly to demanding money under the threat of public exposure. Many victims describe a sense of panic and helplessness, fearing irreparable damage to their personal and professional lives. Criminal gangs, particularly those operating from overseas, are frequently implicated in these schemes. Victims report interactions where they hear multiple voices in the background, indicating that sextortion is often a coordinated effort rather than the work of a lone individual. Platforms like Instagram, Snapchat, WhatsApp, Telegram and dating platforms are commonly used by these offenders, making social media a dangerous breeding ground for such crimes.

Another highly common pattern, predominantly affecting women, features male ex-partners or acquaintances deliberately distributing intimate images as an act of retaliation or control. Many victims describe how their former partners weaponized private content against them, whether by leaking it online, sending it to family members, or using it as blackmail to maintain control over the relationship. For some, the abuse does not stop at the initial sharing; instead, images continue to resurface on multiple platforms, making it an ongoing battle to regain privacy. Offenders often exploit legal loopholes, arguing that the content was initially shared consensually, even though its distribution was not.

Beyond personal retaliation, some offenders use coercion within intimate relationships to manipulate their victims. Threats to release private content unless specific demands are met, whether financial, emotional or sexual, are a recurring theme. Many perpetrators falsely assure victims that images have been deleted, only to later use them as leverage for further control. Victims describe being trapped in cycles of abuse, unable to leave relationships due to the constant fear of exposure. Women, in particular, report threats from male partners who use these images to keep them compliant and submissive, while men experience threats that target their reputations and careers.

Data from the Helpline also sheds light on catfishing and the use of fake online identities as tools for manipulation. In many cases, offenders pretend to be someone else, gaining the trust of victims before pressuring them to share explicit content. Once an image is obtained, the dynamic shifts immediately: what started as a seemingly innocent interaction transforms into threats and blackmail. Victims who initially believed they were engaging in a private exchange suddenly find themselves at the mercy of fraudsters demanding money. These scams are often run by organized criminal groups, particularly in regions such as Nigeria and the Philippines, where perpetrators exploit legal jurisdictional issues that make prosecution difficult.

Another significant trend is hacking and account takeovers, where offenders gain access to a victim's private accounts, steal intimate images, and use them for blackmail or impersonation. Some offenders lock victims out of their accounts entirely, preventing them from removing content or warning others. Victims struggle with regaining control, as social media platforms are often slow to respond to hacking reports, allowing offenders to continue their abuse unchecked.

What makes these crimes even more devastating is the persistence of the offenders. Many victims describe repeated harassment, where offenders return months or even years later with new threats. Some perpetrators create fake social media accounts impersonating their victims, spreading misinformation and further humiliating them in public spaces. Others manipulate the cultural or social vulnerabilities of their victims, particularly in cases of honour-based abuse, where victims fear rejection or violence from their families or communities if their private content is exposed.

In the most extreme cases, victims express suicidal thoughts due to the overwhelming distress caused by this abuse. The emotional and psychological toll is immense, with many individuals losing jobs, relationships and a sense of security in their own lives. Offenders are fully aware of this power dynamic and deliberately prolong the threats to maintain control, ensuring that victims live in a constant state of fear.

Criminal Justice Response

As we have discovered over the ten years of operation of the Helpline, it is often evident that having the legislation is only part of the process of achieving effective outcomes for victims. As the legislation has evolved it is worthwhile to also measure victim outcomes since the inception of the original legislation. The Ministry of Justice publish annual crime

Table 4.1 Ministry of Justice Figures on IIA

	2015	2016	2017	2018	2019	2020	2021	2022	2023
Proceeded against	82	267	306	226	200	186	241	293	324
Convicted	64	228	285	202	178	180	210	256	286
Sentenced	63	228	284	210	181	177	219	261	280
Custody Rate (%)	25.4	22.8	19.0	21.0	21.6	23.2	18.7	23.8	21.1
Average Length (months)	5.3	5.5	5.7	5.9	6.3	7.1	6.6	6.9	7.1

statistics,[8] which allow us to determine the volume of prosecution and conviction and provide a useful tool when considering the efficacy of the law. Below, in Table 4.1, we present prosecution data from 2015 (when the original legislation reached assent and allowed us to measure prosecutions specifically for IIA) to 2023, the most up to date figures we have.

The data on prosecutions for image-based abuse crimes shows several trends which are useful in considering the impact of the legislation. However, we should acknowledge we cannot with this data see which specific piece of legislation has been applied, just that it relates to IIA. Firstly, there is a general increase over time of prosecutions, starting from 82 in 2015 to 324 in 2023. While this suggests a growing recognition of image-based abuse as a criminal issue, possibly influenced by legal reforms and improved enforcement, there is also variation in that time, with decreases as well as increases in prosecution. For example, there are almost as many proceedings in 2017 (306) as there are in 2023 (324).

The number of convictions has followed a similar trend, rising from 64 in 2015 to 286 in 2023, indicating that as more cases are being prosecuted, a consistent proportion still result in convictions, but there is a similar fluctuation during this time and over the majority of this time the number of prosecutions that result in conviction remains at between 85 and 90%, which suggests that when charges against IIA do go to trial,

[8] https://www.gov.uk/government/collections/criminal-justice-statistics. Accessed May 2025.

they are usually successful, the numbers that do move to prosecute are low.

So, we have evidence to show that when complaints result in moves to prosecute, there is a high level of success in achieving a prosecution. However, we know from research around sexual crime in general (for example Taylor & Gassner, 2010) that getting to a decision to prosecute from a complaint can take considerable time and effort, and the figures for number of complaints that become charges are low.

In order to see how low compared to the number of complaints made, we also issued a Freedom of Information request to all forces in England, Wales and Northern Ireland for data on arrests related to IIA in 2023. A Freedom of Information (FOI) request is a formal request for access to information held by public authorities, including government departments, law enforcement agencies, and local councils. Under the Freedom of Information Act 2000 (UK Government, 2000) in the UK, the public has the right to request data and records that are not classified or exempt from disclosure. FOI requests are particularly useful for crime data as they allow us to obtain detailed, unpublished statistics on crime trends, law enforcement actions, and prosecution rates.

In this case we asked:

> *Please could you provide us with the numbers in relation to the following information, for the period 31st January 2023 to 30th January 2024, concerning Disclosing private sexual photographs and films with intent to cause distress under Section 33 of the Criminal Justice and Courts Act (2015) where the victim is aged 18 or older:*

- *Reported cases*
- *Arrests*
- *Outcomes:*
  - *No further action (with further detail, if possible)*
  - *Charges*
  - *Other resolutions*

Police crime outcomes refer to the process by which police forces in the UK categorize the results of reported crimes, indicating how each case was handled and whether a suspect was charged, cautioned, or if no further action was taken. This allows us to explore whether someone is charged because of a complaint and, if not, why the complaint was not taken forward.

43 forces in total were asked to respond, and in total we received 37 responses from forces that represent an approximate overall population of 48,680,000 citizens. Table 4.2 shows a summary of the data collected in an aggregated form.

The data is particularly useful for several reasons. First, the number drawn from 37 forces that resulted in charges (264) is in line with the total number of proceeding against in that year (324 from the Ministry of Justice data). This gives us confidence that the data received is accurate and in line with national statistics.

However, what is perhaps more telling, if we are to consider whether the improvement in legislation, of themselves, has improved outcomes for victims, there is less to support this. Firstly, as we can see from the Ministry of Justice data, there is little change in the number of prosecutions as the legislation improved. And while, as we have already said, there is a high conviction rate for those that move to prosecute, it would seem from the Freedom of Information data that the number that enter

Table 4.2 FOI responses from police forces on IIA actions

Reports	6459
Arrests	1037
OC01 (Charge/Summons)	264
OC03 (Adult Caution)	63
OC05 (Offender has died)	3
OC08 (Community Resolution)	56
OC10 (Not in Public Interest)	20
OC12 (Suspect too ill)	6
OC13 (Prosecution prevented—victim/key witness dead/ill)	2
OC14 (Named suspect not identified/the victim declines/unable to identify offender)	420
OC15 (Insufficient Evidence)	1369
OC16 (Suspect identified but the victim does not/withdraws support for police action)	2180
OC17 (Time Limit Expired)	54
OC18 (No Line of Enquiry)	887
OC20 (Further action undertaken by another body/agency)	42
OC21 (Investigation not in Public Interest)	19
OC22 (Diversionary and/or educational intervention)	28

this part of the justice process is very small compared to the number of complaints received. From the Freedom of Information data, we can see that of complaints made, only 16% will result in an arrest, and of the 1037 arrests made, only 32% will result in a move to prosecute or caution for the offender. Or, if we are to consider complaints against move to prosecute, we can see that only approximately 4% of complaints of IIA reported to the police result in a charge. Which follows a trend around sexual crime complaints rarely resulting in conviction. For example, data from Rape Crisis,[9] a UK-based network of independent charities that provide specialist support, advocacy, and information to survivors of rape, sexual assault, and sexual abuse, indicates that between October 2023 and September 2024, fewer than 3 in 100 rapes recorded by police resulted in a charge within the same year. Perhaps one of the most concerning statistics coming from the Freedom of Information data is that the most likely outcome for a complaint is, in 2180 cases, victim does not support or withdraws support for police action.

Which, once again, goes to confirm that while legislation is a very important part of moving to address the harms of IIA and the impact upon victims it does not, of itself, solve these issues. If other aspects of the criminal justice system, such as prosecutors and police, do not understand the nature of the impact of these crimes on victims, or do not take complaints seriously, there is a significant risk that adding new pieces of legislation will do little to improve outcomes for victims.

As we explore in the following two chapters, support for victims from the ecosystem can be inconsistent and effective legal recourse requires the involvement of many stakeholders in the criminal justice system. Or, to put it another way, having effective legalization that understands the nature of the crime and impact on victims, is only one part of the ecosystem. Which, of itself, does raise concerns around the direction of travel for more recent policy developments around dealing with NCII.

---

[9] https://rapecrisis.org.uk/get-informed/statistics-sexual-violence/. Accessed May 2025.

Policy Hyperactivity

In the last six months (given this book was written in January to May 2025), there has been a lot more focus on IIA across the regulatory space, which is undoubtedly a positive thing, but with the focus returning to illegality and *platform liability*. While some of this is to be welcomed, it is perhaps disheartening to see that legislation and platforms are the focus, rather than awareness, education and training. While, clearly, it is important that NCII is made illegal, and effectively so, we also know from many other areas of social policy, such as road traffic regulation and tackling drug harms, making something illegal does not make these issues go away [refs]. They are a useful starting point, and an important aspect of victim support, but not a solution.

What is clearly evident from the recent Ministry of Justice and Freedom of Information data is that (as with a lot of sexual crimes) the number of victims who receive recompense from the justice system is tiny, and the data would suggest the flaws lie in the criminal justice process as well as legislation. There is a risk of *policy hyperactivity* around these issues, with a rush to introduce new legislation without tackling the flaws in the ecosystem. This is something that can be attributed to online safety law in general (Phippen, 2025), but there is a risk similar might take place around NCII, which is a particular concern given the obsession with platform liability that underpins recent online safety legislative efforts (ibid.). The issues around platform liability as a "solution" to NCII are discussed in more detail in Chapter 6, where we explore what is, and what is not, possible with technological intervention in this domain.

The Non-Consensual Sexually Explicit Images and Videos (Offences) Bill,[10] introduced by Baroness Owen of Alderley Edge in September 2024 and at the time of writing working through the parliamentary process, represents a significant step towards criminalizing both the non-consensual capture of intimate images and the creation of digitally fabricated content, such as deepfake pornography. The Bill aims to make it illegal to take, solicit, or produce sexually explicit images or videos

---

[10] https://bills.parliament.uk/bills/3759. Accessed May 2025.

of another person without their consent, addressing a long-standing gap in the law. Offenders could face imprisonment or fines, though debates over the severity of penalties have emerged during the legislative process. While the Bill has received broad support, government proposals to introduce weaker penalties—limited to fines and subject to a "reasonable excuse" defence—have been met with criticism for being too lenient.

Recent policy discussions have also emphasized the criminalization of new forms of image-based abuse, particularly in response to the rise of AI-generated intimate images and deepfake pornography. The Crime and Policing Bill 2025[11] introduces new offences that make it illegal to capture intimate images or install equipment for this purpose without consent, further closing legal loopholes that previously allowed such activities to go unpunished. Additionally, amendments under the Data (Use and Access) Bill[12] propose criminalizing the creation of "purported sexual images", ensuring that AI-generated intimate content falls within the scope of criminal law. These legislative changes reflect ongoing efforts to expand legal protections, recognizing that current laws are insufficient in tackling emerging forms of intimate image abuse.

The broader pornography regulation debate has also focused on strengthening legal accountability rather than relying solely on education or law enforcement improvements. The consultation document "Creating a Safer World—The Challenge of Regulating Online Pornography"[13] emphasizes that platform regulation is the most immediate and effective approach to reducing harm. It calls for stricter legal measures such as mandatory content moderation, increased penalties for non-compliance, and independent audits of pornography platforms. Additionally, new proposals suggest business disruption measures to remove harmful content, a ban on "nudification" apps, and compulsory AI tools to detect and eliminate non-consensual pornography (see Chapter 7 for more discussion on the efficacy of AI for these social harms). The Online Safety Act 2023 has already designated intimate image abuse as a "priority offence", but policymakers argue that criminalizing additional

[11] https://bills.parliament.uk/bills/3938. Accessed May 2025.

[12] https://bills.parliament.uk/bills/3825. Accessed May 2025.

[13] https://www.gov.uk/government/publications/creating-a-safer-world-the-challenge-of-regulating-online-pornography. Accessed May 2025.

offences, such as the creation of non-consensual content, is necessary to close remaining legal gaps.

Despite these legal advancements, the pattern of continuous legislative change persists, with policymakers repeatedly asserting that current laws are inadequate and need further strengthening. While legal reforms are essential to criminalize new forms of intimate image abuse, the recurring theme of "the laws are not strong enough, we need better ones" raises questions about whether legislative measures alone can effectively deter offenders and prevent abuse.

Women and Equalities Committee Report on NCII 2025

In drawing these legal and policy discussions to a close, for now, we acknowledge the recent publication of the Women and Equalities Committee's report on non-consensual intimate image abuse (NCII) (Women & Equalities Committee, 2025) which highlights significant gaps in the legal and regulatory framework but also acknowledges that the ecosystem, and the stakeholders within it, need to improve victim support.

Despite the introduction of the Online Safety Act 2023, which criminalizes NCII and places obligations on online platforms, enforcement remains a challenge, particularly against non-compliant websites hosted overseas. The report identifies a major flaw in the current legislation: while the act of creating and sharing NCII is illegal, possessing such material is not, meaning platforms and individuals are not legally compelled to remove or refrain from storing it. Additionally, the government has yet to introduce a civil legal framework that would allow victims to swiftly secure takedown orders or seek compensation. While there have been politcal calls, including in this report, that "NCII should be treated the same as Child Sexual Abuse Material (CSAM)", which is difficult to disagree with, the nature of NCII compared to CSAM makes this challenging if left to service providers to address. This is a challenging issue that is explored in more detail in Chapter 6.

However, unlike some of the other policy discussions at the present time around NCII, this report is keen to raise concerns around victim support around the ecosystem as a whole. Victims of NCII abuse continue to face re-traumatization when seeking justice. Many have reported poor treatment by the police, with some being advised to keep their NCII online as evidence for court cases. Furthermore, victims are frequently denied financial support, as NCII is not classified as a violent crime under the Criminal Injuries Compensation Scheme (CICS). The report highlights that services such as the Revenge Porn Helpline, have seen a surge in demand but remain underfunded, operating at 2020 budget levels despite a sevenfold increase in cases.

The report discusses how many victims face barriers to justice due to statutory time limits, which often expire before they even become aware of the abuse. Even when cases are reported, police failures—including delays, lack of training, and instances of misogyny—further undermine victims' ability to seek redress. The report highlights that some victims have only discovered their abuse through media reports, suggesting a failure in police notification and response. Additionally, survivors frequently experience re-traumatization, with some being advised not to take their images down to preserve evidence for lengthy legal proceedings. Inadequate sanctions against perpetrators also exacerbate harm, as convicted offenders are sometimes allowed to retain devices containing NCII content, further violating victims' privacy.

The report is critical of the regulator, Ofcom and states that it lacks the authority to intervene directly on behalf of individuals, unlike the Australian eSafety Commissioner, which can compel platforms and ISPs to remove NCII content. Moreover, victims seeking justice through civil litigation often face high costs and complex legal barriers, as existing laws—such as defamation and harassment claims—are not tailored to NCII cases. The report urges the Government to introduce a dedicated civil legal process, like models in Canada and the USA, which would allow victims to secure compensation, require content deletion, and obtain "Take Down" court orders. Additionally, the report calls for expanding the legal definition of NCII to include culturally intimate content, such as images of individuals without religious attire, which can have severe social and emotional consequences.

Beyond legal gaps, insufficient funding for victim support services remains a pressing concern. The Revenge Porn Helpline, a crucial resource for victims, has experienced a sevenfold increase in cases over the past four years, yet government funding has remained stagnant since 2020. Meanwhile, some major tech companies, such as Google, have not yet implemented hashing technology to block NCII, despite using similar tools for child sexual abuse material. The report calls for urgent, multi-year funding to ensure services can keep pace with the growing technical sophistication and volume of NCII abuse. It also recommends stronger enforcement mechanisms, including blocking access to non-compliant websites, and establishing an Online Safety Commission to act as a trusted intermediary for victims, ensuring swifter and more effective content removal. Without these systemic changes, the report warns that victims will continue to suffer lifelong consequences, while perpetrators and non-compliant platforms exploit legal and regulatory loopholes with impunity.

Conclusions

The evolution of the UK's legislative response to intimate image abuse (IIA) over the past decade represents a considerable shift in how digital sexual harms are recognized in law. From the introduction of the *Criminal Justice and Courts Act 2015* to more recent developments under the *Online Safety Act 2023*, lawmakers have taken substantial steps towards criminalizing a broader range of behaviours—from threats and voyeurism to deepfakes and cyberflashing. On paper, the legislative landscape has become increasingly comprehensive.

However, this chapter has demonstrated that legal reform, while necessary, is not in itself sufficient. Despite expanded definitions and new offences, many victims still do not achieve justice. Only a fraction of complaints progress to charges or convictions. Most cases are closed with no further action, often because victims withdraw or because the investigative and prosecutorial systems are unequipped, untrained, or under-resourced to handle these complex and deeply personal crimes.

The gap between the existence of laws and the effective enforcement of those laws remains stark.

The case studies discussed—spanning high-profile figures like Georgia Harrison and Zara McDermott to anonymous survivors like "Victoria"—highlight both the long-term psychological toll of IIA and the barriers victims face when seeking redress. These cases show that survivors often want something far simpler than a courtroom win: they want their images removed, their privacy restored, and their autonomy respected. Yet current systems still too often fail to deliver even these basic outcomes.

One of the most consistent themes throughout this chapter is the role of the *Revenge Porn Helpline* (RPH) in shaping the legislative journey. Not only has the Helpline provided direct support to tens of thousands of victims, but it has also produced a body of evidence that has proven indispensable to policymakers, regulators, and campaigners. Through Freedom of Information requests, case analysis, and consultation responses, RPH has helped to identify legislative blind spots, test new processes, and challenge assumptions about how these crimes affect victims. Their influence can be seen across almost every major reform in the last ten years—including the criminalization of threats to share, the recognition of deepfakes, and the removal of the intent requirement in the most recent legislation.

However, the data is clear: prosecutions remain low, conviction rates steady but rare, and withdrawal of victim support is common. As such, we must confront the limitations of relying solely on legal reform to deliver justice. True progress requires systemic change across the entire victim-support ecosystem-policing, prosecutions, platforms, mental health services, and public awareness. The recent *Women and Equalities Committee* report rightly acknowledges that without a properly resourced infrastructure-one that includes civil redress, education, platform accountability, and robust victim support-laws risk becoming symbolic gestures rather than functional protections.

As policy momentum around NCII continues to build, there is a risk of legislative overreach or performative regulation that fails to address the practical needs of victims. The voices captured in this chapter—whether shared through Helpline messages, courtroom testimony, or public advocacy—remind us that legal tools must be grounded in the lived realities of those they aim to protect. If victims are to regain control of their images, their narratives, and their futures, then legislation must be matched with meaningful support, cultural change, and institutional empathy.

The next chapters will explore more deeply the nature of IIA and the breadth of behaviours and impacts therein, and the broad IIA ecosystem and the impact of stakeholders in this space.

References

Phippen, A. (2025). *Policy and rights challenges in children's online behaviour and safety, 2017–2023.* Springer Nature Switzerland.

Skočir, M. (2024). Governing digital spaces: Addressing illegal and harmful user-generated content on online platforms. *Revija za kriminalistiko in kriminologijo/Ljubljana, 75*(4), 290–303.

Taylor, S. C., & Gassner, L. (2010). Stemming the flow: Challenges for policing adult sexual assault with regard to attrition rates and under-reporting of sexual offences. *Police Practice and Research: An International Journal, 11*(3), 240–255.

UK Government. (2000). *Freedom of Information Act 2000.* https://www.legislation.gov.uk/ukpga/2000/36. Accessed May 2025.

UK Government. (2015). *Criminal Justice and Courts Act 2015, c. 2, § 33.* https://www.legislation.gov.uk/ukpga/2015/2/section/33. Accessed May 2025.

UK Government. (2016). *Abusive Behaviour and Sexual Harm Act (Scotland).* https://www.legislation.gov.uk/asp/2016/22/section/2. Accessed May 2025.

UK Government. (2021). *Domestic Abuse Act 2021: Section 69*. Legislation.gov.uk. https://www.legislation.gov.uk/ukpga/2021/17/section/69/enacted. Accessed May 2025.

UK Government. (2023). *Online Safety Act 2023.* https://www.legislation.gov.uk/ukpga/2023/50. Accessed May 2025.

Véliz, C. (2019). The internet and privacy. In *Ethics and the contemporary world* (pp. 149–159). Routledge.

Welsh, K. (2025). The Online Safety Act 2023: A new dawn for regulating image-based domestic abuse?. In *Victimisation in the digital age* (pp. 121–136). Routledge.

West, J. R. (2024). Image-based sexual violence and imperfect victims: The case for platform cooperativism in the online sex industry. *Porn Studies*, 1–15.

Women and Equalities Committee. (2025). *Tackling non-consensual intimate image abuse*. https://publications.parliament.uk/pa/cm5901/cmselect/cmwomeq/336/report.html. Accessed May 2025.

5

Nuance and Context in Intimate Image Abuse

Abstract This chapter expands on the victim-centred focus of prior analysis by challenging oversimplified narratives around Intimate Image Abuse (IIA) and exploring its deeply contextual, multifaceted nature. Drawing on extensive data from the UK's Revenge Porn Helpline, it highlights the diversity of victims and perpetrators, as well as the varying forms and impacts of abuse, including sextortion, voyeurism, synthetic sexual content, and honour-based threats. The chapter critically examines how gender, age, culture, and technology intersect to shape victim experiences and reveals stark disparities in harm: women are disproportionately affected by the sharing of images, while men are more commonly targeted by sextortion. Legal definitions of "intimacy" are shown to be culturally limited, failing to account for contexts where non-sexual images can trigger social ostracism or violence. The chapter also evaluates global and national legislative responses, acknowledging progress but emphasizing the urgent need for consistency, international cooperation, and systemic reform across the justice system. Ultimately, it argues for a nuanced, culturally aware, and survivor-informed approach to effectively support all victims of IIA.

S. Mortimer et al., *Ten Years of the Revenge Porn Helpline*, Palgrave Studies in Victims and Victimology, https://doi.org/10.1007/978-3-032-00614-1_5

Keywords Contextual victimization · Gendered digital abuse · Cultural harm disparities · Sextortion and synthetic content · Global and legal inconsistencies

Discussions around intimate image abuse (IIA) often begin with a deceptively simple question: *What does a typical victim look like?* But as this chapter will explore, that question is not only unhelpful—it is deeply misleading. There is no single profile, no consistent narrative, no standard experience. The abuse can happen to anyone, and it *does* happen to people across every age group, gender, background, and belief system. Understanding IIA requires us to go far beyond headlines and legal definitions, and instead to reckon with the complex social, emotional, and technological realities that shape how abuse occurs, how victims are harmed, and how they can—or cannot—seek redress.

This chapter builds on the legal and victim-centred focus of Chapter 4 by zooming out and diving deeper into the messy, shifting landscape of IIA as it is *actually experienced*. Using data and casework from the Revenge Porn Helpline, we examine the diversity of victims, perpetrators, and abuse patterns, and how these are shaped by gender, age, culture, technology, and socio-political context. From sextortion scams targeting young men to coercive control within intimate relationships, from voyeurism to synthetic sexual content, from online sex work to honour-based abuse—each instance reveals how varied, and deeply contextual, this form of harm truly is.

This chapter challenges assumptions and highlights where common narratives fall short. It addresses the gendered nature of harm-why women's images are shared far more often than men's, and why male victims often face uniquely shaming forms of extortion. It interrogates cultural blind spots in legal definitions, such as what counts as an "intimate" image in communities where modesty or religious norms drastically alter the meaning of exposure. And it calls attention to the structural inequalities that shape whether a victim feels safe enough to seek help at all.

Ultimately, this chapter argues that a one-size-fits-all response to intimate image abuse is not only ineffective but actively harmful. If we are to respond with justice, care, and effectiveness, we must understand IIA as a layered, context-dependent phenomenon-one shaped not just by technology or law, but by power, gender, culture, and trust. This is a chapter about complexity, but more importantly, it is a call to resist simplification and embrace the nuance necessary to support all victims of this deeply personal, deeply invasive form of abuse.

A Typical Victim

One of the questions we are regularly asked about the Helpline's experience of intimate image abuse is: What is a typical victim? That's a dangerous question, because it suggests that this form of abuse only happens to a certain type of person and if you're not that sort of person then it probably won't happen to you. But intimate image abuse can happen to pretty much anyone, and it does. We are unable to support minors because of the significant difference in legal position of nude or sexual images of minors, but that doesn't stop them contacting us directly or a parent getting in touch on their behalf. We are fortunate to have fantastic partners in this space, the support network for children and young people being so much more mature than that for adults.

Demographic information is always difficult for us to collect. The people that come to us are understandably reluctant to share any information about themselves at all. Just imagine: pictures of you naked or having sex are being shared online, how do you feel about saying where you live or how old you are? We know how important this information is, to *us* to help us understand the victim experience so we can improve our support response; to *academics* for accurate research; for *government* and *funders* to inform policy and legislative change. But while we encourage people to share the information, we don't do any more than that. Limited demographic information means we can't give precise data, but we have enough to illustrate the real experiences of people reporting intimate image abuse.

In 2018, 60% of clients who indicated their age band were aged between 18 and 34; but 28% were aged between 35 and 54 with just above 5% in the over 55 category. Since then, the percentage of people sharing that they were in the younger age group has risen and in the older has dropped: in 2023 almost 79% were in the younger age group and less than 20% in the mid-range. But 2024 saw another shift with those two age groups becoming 71% and 18% respectively.

Similarly, statistics on the gender of clients fluctuate over the years. Overall, 47% of clients have identified themselves as female, with 35% identified as male. In the earlier years of the Helpline's history, this broke down to 60 to 65% female and 20 to 27% male. But more recently we have recorded a shift down to barely 40% female and up to 45% male. Alongside this there has been a sharp rise in the proportion of cases where the gender of the client is unknown, distorting the overall picture: again, in the early years this was less than 10% but more recently has risen to around 20%. The reality is that men and women experience intimate image abuse very differently and in ways that have changed over time, as they will undoubtedly continue to do. To understand more clearly what this looks like, we will have to go further into the data than just the headlines.

The Sharing of Intimate Images Without Consent

When it became a criminal offence to share intimate images without consent, and when the Helpline started, in 2015, the assumption was that this issue would occur in the context of a romantic relationship that had broken down. One party (probably a man) would, through anger or a desire for retribution, share private sexual images of his former partner (probably a woman) with the intention of causing her harm. And there is no doubt that what we frequently see is private images of women being shared by former male partners. Where the issue being reported to us is images being shared, victims are consistently in the region of 75% female. Female victims, where the perpetrator is known, have a male perpetrator almost 85% of the time; for male victims, the perpetrator is a woman only 8% of the time.

Many victims describe how their former partners weaponize their intimate content against them, whether by leaking it online, sending it to family members, or using it as blackmail to maintain control over the relationship. And for many, the abuse does not stop at the initial sharing: their images continue to resurface across multiple platforms, making it an ongoing battle to regain privacy.

Threats to Share Intimate Images

As we have discussed in previous chapters, threats to share intimate images only became a specific criminal offence in 2021 as a result of the Domestic Abuse Act (UK Government, 2021). Until then, it was only possible potentially to prosecute the behaviour via existing laws on harassment or malicious communications, but in practice these were not effective. In 2020, Refuge published *The Naked Threat* report[1] which found that 1 in 14 adults in England and Wales had experienced threats to share intimate images without consent. Again, the behaviour was more common in younger age groups with 60% aged 39 or under. Helpline data reported, in 2020, that 14% of cases included threats to share, with 66% of women reporting a male perpetrator and only 6% a female perpetrator. Male victims reported male perpetrators 28% of the time and female 20%. In 2024, 9.5% of clients reported threats to share intimate images, with nearly 78% of clients being female, with 78% of those perpetrators being male. Of the male victims, 29% reported a male perpetrator and 38% reported a female perpetrator.

Many cases featuring men reporting threats to share intimate images are in the context of a relationship breakdown, where the perpetrators and ex partners are both male and female. There are also multiple cases where the threats are coming from a partner's former partner or an affair partner's spouse or partner. We also regularly see threats to share made from someone that the client met on a meet-up site such as Grindr.

Many female victims reporting threats to share are being threatened by a current or former partner. Often, a current partner is threatening to share the images to coerce the woman to stay in a relationship with them. If the relationship has already broken down, there is a strong

---

[1] https://refuge.org.uk/wp-content/uploads/2020/07/The-Naked-Threat-Report.pdf.

desire from the ex-partner to punish and humiliate: "I will make you go viral" and "I will destroy you". These threats can be long-lasting and have a devastating impact. Often the target is specific, with images being threatened to be shared with friends or family to have great personal impact, or in workplaces to affect jobs and careers. People who work in teaching, nursing or childcare can have significant concerns at the impact of intimate content being shared with work colleagues and management.

We also frequently support women from cultural and religious backgrounds where the consequences of this form of abuse can be even more significant. For many of these women, the sharing of an intimate image, or one that shows a form of behaviour condemned within that community, can put the victim at risk of honour-based abuse and violence.

Voyeurism

A constant thread running through the cases on the Helpline is voyeurism, which is the *taking* of intimate images of someone without their knowledge or consent. Despite this having been a long-standing sexual offence under the Sexual Offences Act 2003, clients are very often unaware that what has happened is against the law and often only mention in passing when reporting the sharing of the images that they had not been aware that they had been created. While voyeurism is reported in 2% of cases, it is inevitable that the true prevalence is much higher just from the nature of the behaviour. Clients report this as being incredibly violating, understandably given the complete side-stepping of the need for consent.

In 2019, the government created new voyeurism offences with the passing of the Voyeurism (Offences) Act 2019 (UK Government, 2019). This act made it a criminal offence to take an image of someone under their clothing without consent, a crime commonly referred to as either "upskirting" or "down-blousing". (For the avoidance of doubt, the legislation is not gendered: it does capture a man in a skirt or kilt and, of course, the perpetrator can be a woman. However, the vast majority of cases reported involve a female victim and male offender.) Original voyeurism offences had not considered the upcoming ubiquity of phones with cameras in everyone's pockets, so up until this point, this behaviour had not been a criminal offence. It only became a specific offence in 2019 as a result of a vigorous campaign by Gina Martin who was upskirted at a music festival in Hyde Park in 2018 (Martin, 2019). She caught a man taking a picture up her skirt, snatched it and ran to a police officer, only to be told that it was not actually a crime in itself but could potentially be caught as "outraging public decency". Martin was appalled that the law as it stood took no account of her as a victim, just the impact on those who had witnessed it happening.

There is no doubt that this is a crime that happens far more often than we realize: the nature of it means that most women simply do not know it has happened. But the proliferation of categories on adult sites of categories called "upskirting" and "creep shots" suggests it is not a niche interest.

Unauthorized Access and Hacking

Clients frequently report that their computers, phones, and accounts have been "hacked" and their intimate content shared as a result. This is often at the hands of partners or friends/family members who gain access to a device and then guess passwords or access a phone which then gives access to photos, social media accounts, emails, and other storage. Some offenders lock victims out of their accounts entirely, preventing them from removing content or warning others. Victims struggle with regaining control, as social media platforms are often slow to respond to hacking reports, allowing offenders to continue their abuse unchecked. However, it is also common that people who have had their intimate images shared *believe* that it has happened because of hacking by a stranger rather than as a result of the person they shared images with privately breaking that trust. Unfortunately, it often becomes apparent that the images have in fact been shared by that person, not via a hacking.

In 2014, a large number of intimate images, mostly of actors, models and celebrities, the vast majority women, were shared online via a hack on iCloud in what became known as the "fappening" (Massanari, 2017).

Thousands of images and videos of some of the most famous women in the world were suddenly widely available on sites and message boards dedicated to this form of content and then seeped to mainstream social media. As time has passed, cloud storage security has improved but leaks of images via hacking have continued. And sites have continued to emerge that specialize in images of celebrities. Of course, the most high-profile victims have access to significant resources that enable them to get most of this content removed and hidden, but those resources are not available to everyone. It has been common over the years for the Helpline to be contacted by people who have had past careers as models or on reality TV shows or talent contests and have then been targeted by a hack with their images uploaded to a dedicated site. It is usually easy to tell that this content has been hacked because it appears as a dump of an entire camera roll, not a curated selection of images. Unfortunately, there are many so-called "celebrity" sites that specialize in this sort of content and do not respond to take down requests. This therefore has a long-term, debilitating effect on victims/survivors, knowing that their images continue to circulate and on sites that use high-profile names to attract clicks and views which inevitably leads to images being downloaded and reshared elsewhere and so it goes on. One client we have been reporting for has had hundreds of images reported, removed and reshared in a continuing cycle that is exhausting and devastating for her and never-ending for the Helpline team.

Content Creators and Online Sex Workers

The law in the UK on the sharing of intimate images without consent specifically excludes professional content or images that have been put online by someone themselves or for financial reward. As such, it falls outside the official remit of the Helpline, but people experiencing this often come to us for help and advice. Frequently, this occurs because someone who has paid for the content chooses to reshare it to others. This would constitute a copyright issue and many sites will offer advice to the creators affected. Sometimes this content is shared to cause harm to a specific content creator, to "out" her amongst family and friends or in her community. In these circumstances, we may be able to offer some advice via our Report Harmful Content service as it may be harassment. We also see private content being shared on professional or subscription sites without the consent of someone in the images, as happened to Georgia Harrison (see Chapter 4). This would be classed as intimate image abuse and we are able to give support. Some subscription sites now have improved procedures for ensuring that everyone in the images shared has given consent, but not all.

Sextortion

One of the most common forms of intimate image abuse that we see on the Helpline, representing between a quarter and a third of cases in recent years, is sextortion, or financially motivated sexual extortion (FMSE) (Ray & Henry, 2025). Unlike the other forms of abuse that are reported to us, sextortion is experienced predominantly by men. Since 2022, over 90% of the clients reporting sextortion to the Helpline are male. The abuse has manifested consistently for as long as the Helpline has been operating: the targets are usually younger men, they are approached by what appears to be a young attractive woman, often on a dating site or social media such as Instagram, the conversation is flirtatious and the woman will suggest moving to a different app for a video call. The call becomes sexual very quickly and then abruptly the victim will be told that the interaction has been recorded, lists of friends and contacts have been captured and demands for money start. Sometimes the scammer will send screenshots of the content back to the victim, sometimes doctored to make it look like the victim was engaging with a child. The demands for money will be repeated and urgent, with victims given a very short amount of time to pay. This is intentional to keep victims panicked and stopping them from taking time to think or get help or advice. Many victims do pay, though may negotiate a reduced amount; paying once, unfortunately, almost guarantees they will be back for more.

Organized criminal gangs, particularly those operating in Nigeria, the Philippines, and parts of Eastern Europe, have turned sextortion into a highly organized financial scheme, specifically targeting victims in wealthier countries.[2] One victim in the case data reported that he was blackmailed into paying over £2,000, only to have the threats continue. Another stated that even after paying, the perpetrators kept demanding more money, making it clear that compliance only fuels further extortion. Unlike other forms of intimate image abuse, which is often personal and focused on control, sextortion by criminal networks is purely transactional. The globalization of digital crime has made it easier for these groups to target victims across borders, leaving law enforcement agencies struggling to intervene effectively. However, the impact of sextortion can be devastating and some clients report worsened mental health and depression or suicidal ideation.

Women do experience sextortion though it often presents differently and would be classed as a "romance scam". This is where a woman has met a man online and is in the belief that she is in a genuine relationship that comes to involve the handing over of money. If the woman starts to become suspicious, this can be where threats to share intimate content can be made.

For clarity, the Helpline advises anyone affected by sextortion to Stop, Block and Report: Stop communication with the scammer; Block them from contact; and Report the accounts to the platform. Do not pay any money, they will just come back for more. The reality is that each scammer with be targeting multiple victims at once and if they are blocked, they will probably just move on to someone else. It is also very rare in our experience that images are shared in sextortion cases. We always encourage victims to report to the police, though in practice, there is little that they can do: the gangs carrying out these operations are based overseas, most commonly in the Philippines, Nigeria, and Morocco, but reporting helps provide additional intelligence. Concerns have also been raised recently at the increased targeting of children by these gangs as reported by the IWF[3] leading to a heightened response from the National Crime Agency, including the issuing of a national alert in April 2024.[4]

---

[2] https://www.bbc.co.uk/news/av/magazine-37705678. Accessed May 2025.

[3] https://www.iwf.org.uk/news-media/news/iwf-urges-young-people-to-get-help-as-criminals-target-younger-children-in-sextortion-scams/.

[4] https://www.nationalcrimeagency.gov.uk/news/nca-issues-urgent-warning-about-sextortion.

Synthetic Sexual Content

Synthetic sexual content (Umbach et al., 2024) is the term that we use at the Helpline to describe sexual images of someone that have been created by the use of AI-generative technologies: images that are commonly known as "deepfakes". We took the decision to stop referring to "deepfakes" in 2024 for similar reasons as to why we don't talk about "revenge porn". The term "deepfake" was coined in 2017 by a Reddit user who was a creator of synthetic sexual content, he had created a space on the platform where he shared sexual content that had been created using face-swapping applications. Although the term took hold in the media and wider discussions about the practice, survivors felt increasingly uncomfortable with a term that originated from a perpetrator. As a support service for victims and survivors, it was appropriate for us to shift terminology. Other phrases also circulate such as "sexual digital forgeries" or "digital fakes".

The Helpline started to receive reports of such content as early as 2017 but in tiny numbers and, in fact, they were often images created by applications such as Photoshop rather than more sophisticated technologies. But the term was pervasive early on. Since then, the numbers reported to the Helpline have stayed very small, only moving into double figures in 2020, where they remain. But just because reports are low doesn't mean that the content doesn't exist: we know that it does because we see it when we're reporting other images, and we see the sites that host it and the categories that have appeared on more mainstream adult sites. The software and applications to create these images have both proliferated and become much easier to use. Something that used to take a reasonable amount of technical knowledge and a quantity of images of someone can now be created in seconds with a user-friendly app and as little as one single image of someone.

There is a school of thought that synthetic sexual content is not as harmful as genuine NCII. Indeed, I have heard it argued that it is *preferable* for these images to be created as a means for men to fulfil their sexual fantasies without using genuine images. But this would be wholly wrong. Victims report impacts on their emotional and psychological wellbeing on a par with those experiencing other forms of intimate image abuse;

they feel disempowered, their bodily autonomy stripped away, reduced to objects. One survivor of this abuse, Jodie (not her real name) has campaigned extensively on the issue, having experienced this content being created and shared of her by her supposed best friend.[5] She has described eloquently the impact of this abuse: "When I first discovered that someone close to me had solicited the creation of deepfake images and videos of me, it shattered my sense of self and safety. It was a devastating reminder that this abuse can be perpetrated by anyone, for any reason".[6]

As these technologies improve and their availability spreads, research into the phenomenon is starting to catch up. And what is abundantly clear is how gendered this form of abuse is: in 2019, cybersecurity company Deeptrace released research[7] that revealed that 96% of this content was pornographic, and almost entirely of women. In 2023, further research from Security Hero[8] showed that the total number of "deepfake" videos online had increased by 550% since 2019; pornography made up 98% of the synthetic content online and 99% of the individuals targeted were women.

When the original legislation criminalizing the sharing of private sexual images without consent was passed in 2015, it specifically excluded images that had been manipulated to appear sexual. This only changed in 2024 with new laws that became part of the Sexual Offences Act 2003 which included "a photograph or film which shows, or appears to show, another person (B) in an intimate state" (UK Government, 2023). Both the previous and current governments have made commitments to legislate on the *creation* of synthetic sexual content, but at the time of writing, it has not been passed.

[5] https://www.bbc.co.uk/news/uk-68673390. Accessed May 2025.

[6] https://www.glamourmagazine.co.uk/article/deepfake-abuse-government-new-laws-jodie. Accessed May 2025.

[7] https://www.bbc.co.uk/news/technology-49961089. Accessed May 2025.

[8] https://www.securityhero.io/state-of-deepfakes/. Accessed May 2025.

What Is an "Intimate" Image?

We discussed in Chapter 3 the definition of a "private, sexual image" as covered by the Criminal Justice and Courts Act 2015, s 33 (UK Government, 2015) and the amendments to the Sexual Offences Act 2003 courtesy of the Online Safety Act 2023 (ibid.). These changes saw a welcome broadening of the definition of what constitutes an intimate image, but it is still a very Westernized definition that ignores swathes of the globe, and communities within the UK, that have different cultural standards. Because the word "intimacy" means different things in different communities, and it is important that we acknowledge and respect those differences.

In 2024, the Helpline supported 30 women who identified themselves as being from a strict religious community and who reported the use of their images by current or former partners. Some of these images were sexual in nature and being used either to threaten compliance within a marriage, or by an ex-partner in an act of perceived retribution. But in most cases, the images themselves were neither nude nor sexual, and would not meet the current legal standard. These images showed a woman who would be expected to wear specific clothing such as a hijab, without it. Or sitting with a man they shouldn't be with. Or ordinary images of them shared on an adult site next to pornographic photos and videos.

The impact of the sharing of such images should not be underestimated. Every woman that reported this form of abuse to the Helpline cited concerns about the impact on her should her family find out about, or view, the images. They referenced potential punishments, breakdown of family relationships, forced marriage and honour-based violence: regardless of how the images originated or were shared, they are viewed as a moral failing on the part of the victim. In one case reported to the Helpline, a woman's ex-husband shared intimate images of her with her family three days into her new marriage causing an immediate divorce. Her family rejected her and she was left isolated and emotionally devastated. These pressures make it impossible for victims to obtain support for fear of the consequences. Examples such as these demonstrate differences in the way victims of intimate image abuse experience harm: while victims in Westernized communities often face public shame and professional consequences, they are generally not at risk of social ostracization or physical retaliation from their families. This difference highlights how cultural attitudes towards sexuality, honour and gender roles shape the experience of victims in profound ways.

What's the Harm?

The harm of intimate image abuse reaches into every part of a victim's life, but the multiple variables of increasing forms of this abuse are affected by age, sex, gender, sexuality, cultural, or religious factors and many others. The forces at play are powerful: people's closest personal relationships, careers and their emotional and psychological wellbeing are impacted by the exposure of their most private areas of life and their sexual expression against the backdrop of structural inequality of the sexes and the sexual double-standard. At the same time, responses from the authorities can be dismissive and undermine the sense of wrong done, while personal and professional relationships are eroded by shame, blame and the humiliation of exposure.

One thing is clear from the ten years of data that we have collected, both quantitative and anecdotal: men and women experience these harms differently. They are affected by the issues in different ways, they have different emotional and psychological responses and they have different impacts.

Over the history of the Helpline, 86% of victims reporting sextortion have been male, and in 2024 that figure was almost 95%. However, of those 1,057 men, only 86, or 8%, had their images shared. And over all issue types, male clients had, on average, 0.33 images shared per person. It is therefore *most* likely that a man will experience sextortion of all forms of this abuse but it is very *unlikely* that he will have his images shared.

Women, on the other hand, experience the sharing of images (61% in 2024), in most cases by a previous or current partner or someone they know. The second largest issue reported was threats to share images (22%), followed by voyeurism (12%) and harassment (10%).

And women are facing the majority of intimate images shared online without their consent: 47% of the women who came to the Helpline in 2024 had images shared, and on average they have had 10.1 images shared each (and this will rise as we continue to report on active cases). For those women, we have (at the time of writing) reported 16,039 images shared without consent, that's 96.5% of the images reported all year. The only good news is that we have, to date, been able to remove 93% of those images.

In 2024, the Helpline started to track reported impacts of the abuse to build evidence for the breadth of harm caused. Over 53% of clients who identified harm, expressed worsened mental health, paranoia, depression or suicidal ideation. 22% identified financial impact or disruption of their working lives. Others reported harassment from other people, relationship breakdown and abuse related to their particular cultural or religious identity. While a small number of men reported depression as a result of their experience, it was more commonly experienced by women; but worsening mental health from a pre-existing condition was more than twice as often reported by women, and suicidal ideation was expressed nearly 50% more by women. While women were more than twice as likely to experience job disruption, men were 13 times more likely to report a financial impact. Women were also twice as likely to experience relationship breakdown and four times as likely to receive harassment from others.

The significance in these differences almost always relates to the images that continue to circulate. As noted above, the vast majority of images that the Helpline reports for removal are of women. In fact, since the Helpline started, 98% of all the images we have reported, have been of women. And while the Helpline has an excellent takedown rate, that still leaves thousands of images that continue to circulate online and that cause ongoing harm. Women have told us how devastating this feels: "The distress this has caused, knowing my photos are still out there and completely out of my control, has been extreme" and "it feels like being violated and humiliated all over again, losing control of my own body".

On the other hand, male victims of sextortion face different cultural barriers. In many parts of the world, masculinity is closely tied to strength and control, making it deeply shameful for a man to admit that he has been manipulated, blackmailed or victimized. The Helpline has seen hundreds of cases of young men who were lured into sending explicit images, only to be blackmailed for money later. Many of them struggled with reporting the crime out of fear of being ridiculed or not taken seriously.

A similar stigma surrounds LGBTQ+ victims, particularly in countries where same-sex relationships are criminalized. Some victims feared that reporting their case might not only expose their images but also their sexual identity, putting them at risk of legal or social persecution. But even in the UK, LGBTQ+ clients express reluctance to report to the police for fear of being outed. A 2016 study from Data & Society in the USA found that LGB internet users were four times more likely than their heterosexual counterparts to have their intimate images shared without their consent.[9] Helpline data does not reflect this disparity which raises concerns that members of this community do not reach out for help and support, likely due to the anticipated repercussions.

What makes these crimes even more devastating is the persistence of the offenders. Many victims describe repeated harassment, where offenders return months or even years later with new threats. Some perpetrators go so far as to create fake social media accounts impersonating their victims, spreading misinformation and further humiliating them in public spaces. Others manipulate the cultural or social vulnerabilities of their victims, particularly in cases of honour-based abuse, where victims fear rejection from their families or communities if their private content is exposed. In the most extreme cases, victims express suicidal thoughts due to the overwhelming distress caused by this abuse. The emotional and psychological toll is immense, with many individuals losing jobs, relationships, and a sense of security in their own lives. Offenders are fully aware of this power dynamic and deliberately prolong the threats to maintain control, ensuring that victims live in a constant state of fear.

The data suggests that while Western societies are more open to discussing digital consent and victim rights, patriarchal or conservative

---

[9] https://datasociety.net/pubs/oh/Nonconsensual_Image_Sharing_2016.pdf.

cultures still place much of the blame on the victim, making it harder for them to seek support.

The Global Legal Picture

Helpline data reveals profound cultural differences in how intimate image abuse is experienced, reported, and responded to by both victims and authorities. While the crime itself, whether sextortion, "revenge porn", or coercive control, follows similar patterns across different regions, its social, legal, and emotional consequences vary significantly depending on cultural norms. And these variations are compounded where the behaviours of this abuse play out across borders. Because the internet largely ignores jurisdictional boundaries and victims can find themselves in a completely different environment from their perpetrator and entirely without legal redress, effective support or access to justice.

Though some countries around the world, including the UK, have strengthened laws in this area in recent years, making it easier for victims to pursue justice and have their content removed, the lack of consistency combined with the nature of the internet has created barriers. In addition, enforcement remains inconsistent and victims frequently report long delays or dismissive attitudes from police officers. By contrast, in many parts of Asia, Africa, and the Middle East, legal protections are either weak or non-existent. In some cases, victims themselves face legal repercussions for being in the images in the first place. This is particularly true in countries with strict morality laws, where a woman in an intimate image might be seen as violating public decency laws, even if the image was obtained through coercion or hacking.

One victim described how she hesitated to report her case to the authorities because she feared that she might be arrested rather than the perpetrator. Another victim, living in a conservative country, knew that police intervention could lead to even greater social consequences, such as being disowned or forced into hiding.

Victims in Western nations generally have more access to support services, legal aid, and advocacy groups, making it easier for them to seek help. However, in many developing nations, the combination of legal ambiguity, victim-blaming, and fear of exposure prevents victims from ever reporting the crime.

International Solutions

At the risk of pointing out the obvious, the internet is global and, if I post a picture on a public page, almost everybody in the world will be able to see it. And this means that we need a level of cooperation globally to manage abuse and harm on the internet beyond anything else. Huge strides have been made in tackling the spread of child sexual abuse material (CSAM) online and terrorist material, which has created footsteps that those of us working to protect adult victims of intimate image abuse can follow, with adjustments. The international community is only at the very start of finding its way, but there have been positive collaborations such as the White House Task Force to Address Online Harassment and Abuse (White House, 2023) and the French Government's Laboratoire pour les droits des femmes en ligne (French Government, 2024).

A challenge with writing about this particular area is that, at present, it rarely stands still and new legislation is emerging all of the time. As of May 2025, the United States has passed the Take It Down Act (US Congress, 2025), the first comprehensive federal legislation aimed at combating non-consensual intimate image (NCII) abuse in the USA. This bipartisan law, supported by Senators Ted Cruz and Amy Klobuchar, criminalizes the knowing distribution or threat to distribute intimate images—including AI-generated "deepfake" content—without the subject's consent. It requires online platforms to remove reported NCII content within 48 hours and eliminate duplicates, with the Federal Trade Commission (FTC) overseeing enforcement under its consumer protection authority. Violators face penalties of up to two years in prison, or three years if the victim is a minor. Supported by major tech companies and First Lady Melania Trump, the Act passed with overwhelming bipartisan support, including a 409-2 vote in the House. While praised for addressing the widespread harm of NCII, the legislation has drawn criticism from civil liberties groups over concerns about potential over-censorship, the risk of misuse through false takedown requests,[10] and the FTC's limited capacity to enforce it.[11] Despite these concerns, the Act marks a pivotal step in US efforts to tackle digital abuse and may set the groundwork for future reforms, particularly as AI-generated content continues to evolve.

These initiatives need to engage closely with organizations globally that work directly with victims and survivors to ensure that policy and legislation are guided by their genuine experiences of abuse. This represents a significant challenge in itself: the majority of these organizations are NGOs, many of them very small and running on limited funding. Many of them focus primarily on domestic abuse or women's equality and don't have expertise in online spaces but have expanded their remits in recognition of women's experiences. Conversely, some NGOs that have specialized in supporting children online, have expanded to include adults as our understanding of the seriousness and extent of the problem has grown. Bringing these disparate entities together to share experience, learning and best practice is one of the focuses of the StopNCII.org initiative: the website lists[12] over 100 charities, CSOs/NGOs and other entities that provide support around the world to people experiencing this abuse.

We need the online platforms that host, share and reshare these images to take responsibility and do whatever they can to make their sites safer places for everyone, to do everything in their power to stop these images being uploaded and to respond swiftly and effectively when a report is made to them for removal. And this cannot simply focus on the big players, the household names of social media. The majority of these have reporting routes and systems to remove these images and concentrating solely on them ignores the smaller, high-risk platforms where this content proliferates.

---

[10] https://apnews.com/article/take-it-down-deepfake-trump-melania-first-amendment-741a6e525e81e5e3d8843aac20de8615. Accessed May 2025.

[11] https://www.washingtonpost.com/politics/2025/04/08/take-it-down-act-deepfakes-ncii-flaws/?utm_source=chatgpt.com. Accessed May 2025.

[12] https://stopncii.org/partners/global-network-of-partners/. Accessed May 2025.

StopNCII.org (see Chapter 7 for further discussion) is the world's first device-side hashing technology, allowing people who are concerned that their intimate images may be shared, to create digital "hashes" of those images on their own devices that will reduce and prevent the spread of those images on partner platforms. And the images never leave the device, prioritizing user privacy on sites that include (at March 2025) Facebook, Instagram, TikTok, Snapchat, Threads, Reddit, and Pornhub. The tool is available to any adult, anywhere in the world 24 hours a day. But because the response to intimate image abuse is voluntary many platforms and search engines choose not to engage.

A significant barrier to effective responses to intimate image abuse for victims is the lack of legislation globally, and the lack of consistency in what exists. The United Nations expects to pass its first comprehensive Convention Against Cybercrime in mid-2025 (United Nations, 2024); Article 16 of the Convention requires that "Each State Party shall adopt such legislative and other measures as may be necessary to establish as criminal offences under its domestic law, when committed intentionally and without right, the selling, distributing, transmitting, publishing or otherwise making available of an intimate image of a person by means of an information and communications technology system, without the consent of the person depicted in the image". Elements of the Article are narrower than we might wish to see, for example, the definition of an intimate image is one where "sexual parts are exposed or the person is engaged in sexual activity", and the Convention allows that a State "may require the intent to cause harm" which the UK experience strongly indicates actively fails victims (see Chapter 4).

The Revenge Porn Helpline has carried out a mapping exercise[13] to illustrate the current level of compliance with the imminent legislation. Of the 195 states surveyed, 100 have no legislation at all and 18 were classed as "insufficient"; only 67 were deemed to have sufficient law. But even those 67 will not necessarily be consistent with each other. However, Article 16 represents a first attempt to achieve a global, legal standard that all member states will be required to adopt and we cannot underestimate its significance.

---

[13] https://swgfl.org.uk/resources/adult-image-based-abuse-model-response/.

But legislation, while crucial, is only the first step: there is no point in having legislation if it is not enforced. And for it to be enforced there needs to be national and international awareness of what the law says; there needs to be an investment in law enforcement and criminal justice infrastructure that facilitates effective investigations and prosecutions; there needs to be support and advocacy for victims who come forward seeking justice and there needs to be proactive and preventative measures to stop the spread of non-consensual images alongside the swift and effective removal of images when shared. Factoring in each country's own political, cultural and religious context, the scale of the challenge is undoubtedly vast, but it is necessary for the protection and dignity of women everywhere.

National Solutions for the UK

Legislation: as discussed in Chapter 3, the UK has, since January 2024, had strong legislation around the sharing of intimate images without consent. However, there remains a patchwork of laws that need improving and pulling together for closely related crimes that fall under the intimate image abuse umbrella. Voyeurism falls under the Sexual Offences Act 2003 but the legislation as it stands was not designed for this digital age. The Law Commission, in its comprehensive review (Law Commission, 2021) of the law in this area published in 2022, made recommendations aligning these laws with the sharing offences. The Government have announced they will include these in the Crime and Policing Bill this year, repealing the existing upskirting offence and creating new offences of taking or recording an intimate film without consent with separate offences for intentions to cause alarm, distress or humiliation or for sexual gratification. They will also include new offences on the installation of equipment for the purpose of committing one of those offences.

The Bill also includes an amendment to the Sentencing Code giving courts the power to deprive an offender of any images related to the conviction and any device on which they were stored. It is believed that this power (a deprivation order) is already available to the courts in relation to the sharing offence, though it appears to be very little used. An investigation by *The Observer*[14] in February 2025 revealed that of 98 cases of intimate image abuse recorded in magistrates' courts in the previous six months, only three had resulted in a deprivation order. In March 2025,[15] the CPS announced that it was updating its guidance which now reads: "In the case of offending involving sharing or threatening to share intimate images, devices used or intended to be used to commit or facilitate this offence are liable to a deprivation order and the prosecutor should remind the court of its powers in this respect. This is particularly important in respect of devices which retain the images which the offender shared or threatened to share". Whether this power can be used to remove images that exist online as well as on an offenders' devices remains to be seen.

The Revenge Porn Helpline raised the issue of devices being returned to perpetrators in July 2024 when a client called and said that her ex-partner, who had shared intimate images of her without consent online, had been convicted and given a suspended sentence, but after the case concluded she was called by the police who advised her that they were now obliged to return the offender's phone and laptop to him which still contained her images. She was rightly appalled, but because the court case had concluded without any order being made, there was nothing that the police or anyone else could do.

If the images on those devices had been of a minor this would not have happened: those devices would have been destroyed and the images would have been searched for, hashed and blocked from being visible. This is because it is against the law to be in possession of child sexual abuse material; however, it is not illegal to be in possession of a non-consensual intimate image of an adult even where there has been a conviction. It cannot be right that a victim of this abuse, who has had their experience acknowledged by a criminal conviction, should not have the same outcome that his or her images are deleted from wherever they

---

[14] https://www.theguardian.com/society/2025/feb/22/revenge-porn-abusers-devices-illicit-images.

[15] https://www.theguardian.com/society/2025/mar/23/prosecutors-told-to-do-more-to-strip-revenge-porn-abusers-of-victim-images.

appear. So, while we welcome the amended guidance regarding deprivation orders, we believe that the Government needs to go further and ensure that the possession of a confirmed NCII image is illegal and that not only devices are destroyed on conviction, but that every step possible is taken to remove those images wherever they appear. The Data (Use and Access) Bill, which is also working its way through Parliament, has a proposed amendment (70) requiring the Secretary of State to prepare a Code of Practice on deprivation orders in all of the intimate image abuse offences which "must include guidance for compelling the deletion of copies of an intimate photograph or film, including physical copies and those held on any device, cloud-based programme, or digital, messaging or social media platform they control" which will give a much more comprehensive response if it passes.

Having good legislation is the obvious starting point to getting better outcomes of intimate image abuse. But we need more than good law, we need follow-through from the whole of the criminal justice system. The police are key to this. In 2024, more than three times as many clients reported a negative experience of reporting to the police as a positive one. They reported that the police officers who dealt with their cases didn't know or understand the law, they displayed victim-blaming attitudes, failed to investigate and relied on victims to provide evidence and identify perpetrators. While the internet has brought a whole new dimension to criminal behaviour and policing responses there is no place for outdated, sexist attitudes and no excuse for a lack of basic care of a victim of crime. We know that many forces in the UK are developing training on digital investigation but there is little consistency. It is essential that comprehensive, victim-focused training is given nationally to policing to ensure that thorough investigations happen and victims are supported to ensure that appropriate convictions happen.

Our criminal justice system has been designed to deal with one crime at a time, as a single event. But intimate image abuse rarely happens in isolation: many victims experience IIA as part of a pattern of coercive control, harassment, or domestic abuse. These cases are often complex, involving multiple incidents both on- and offline; each incident may seem minor, but taken as a collective they can indicate a significant and ongoing, escalating campaign of abuse. As observed in Chapter 3, according to FOI data, a third of cases do not proceed because the victim does not support, or has withdrawn support, for the prosecution. This reflects the dynamics of abusive relationships where victims may be persuaded or intimidated not to support prosecution. This represents a significant barrier, and the culture and practices of the criminal justice system need to evolve to overcome it. With nearly 1 in 6 crimes recorded to the police relating to domestic abuse,[16] change cannot come too soon.

The Crown Prosecution Service must work in tandem with policing to ensure effective prosecutions. We also need clarity and consistency on what constitutes evidence in online cases: sometimes screenshots can be used, sometimes they can't; sometimes content needs to stay live until trial (causing additional trauma and raised likelihood of images being shared further) and sometimes they can be removed. Prosecutors, like police officers, need to understand how to locate, collect and store online evidence securely. And prosecutors need to ensure that orders are made on conviction that will protect victims. And of course, all of these stages need to be quicker, victims shouldn't have to wait months, or sometimes years, for their cases to be resolved.

Victims of crime are entitled to prompt and effective support and access to justice. This means that, in addition to criminal proceedings they need access to holistic support from specialist services that can meet their specific needs. Victims of intimate image abuse are frequently experiencing complicated situations that play out both on- and offline and will require a range of supportive interventions: the Revenge Porn Helpline can support with advice around the sharing of intimate images and support with the removal of online content, but other services may be needed to support with domestic abuse, stalking, hacked or impersonation accounts, mental health services, support specific to the LGBT community, or particular religious communities; the list goes on. All of these services need to be comprehensively and effectively funded, giving investment in services not just short-term sticking plasters.

All stakeholders need to be supported to work together to give comprehensive support: for the police to understand the nature of the

---

[16] https://www.ons.gov.uk/peoplepopulationandcommunity/crimeandjustice/bulletins/domesticabuseinenglandandwalesoverview/november2024#:~:text=Domestic%20abuse%2Drelated%20crimes%20represented,female%20in%20the%20last%20year.

support that is needed and that can be provided to tackle complex and interrelated issues; for services to understand the limitations of police responses; we all need to understand what good evidence looks like. Government need to facilitate this collaborative effort and create a feedback loop as to whether the system is working as it should or whether change is needed: the reality of the online world and evolving harms is that change will need to be quick, and Government will need to be agile, to respond appropriately to support victims.

Conclusion

Helpline case data highlights major differences in how other cultures approach online privacy and digital safety. In countries with high levels of digital literacy, individuals are generally more cautious about privacy settings and cybersecurity measures. They are more likely to recognize red flags in online interactions and to be aware of the legal protections available in case of abuse. By contrast, in countries where technology use has expanded rapidly, particularly in parts of Africa, South Asia, and Latin America, there is often less awareness about online safety and the risks of sharing private content. Some victims expressed shock at being blackmailed, stating that they never expected such a thing to happen to them. This suggests that raising awareness about digital privacy, consent, and cybercrime prevention is critical in regions where internet access has grown faster than public education on these issues.

The dataset makes it clear that intimate image abuse is a global problem, but its impact, legal consequences, and social reactions vary widely depending on culture. In Western societies, victims are more likely to report cases, but they still face challenges in getting legal action and content removal.

In conservative and patriarchal cultures, victims, especially women, often suffer double victimization, facing both public shaming and personal retaliation. LGBTQ+ victims in restrictive countries are often too afraid to report abuse, fearing that exposure might lead to further discrimination or criminal charges. Sextortion gangs in low-income countries have turned intimate image abuse into an organized industry, preying on victims from wealthier nations.

Legal loopholes, cultural stigma, and weak enforcement make justice difficult to obtain in many countries. Addressing intimate image abuse effectively requires a culturally informed approach. Solutions must consider regional differences in victim experiences, social attitudes towards privacy and sexuality, and legal protections available to victims. Expanding global awareness, strengthening laws, and fostering cultural shifts towards victim protection rather than victim-blaming will be essential in tackling this growing digital crime.

References

French Government. (2024). *The Laboratory for Women's Rights Online*. https://www.diplomatie.gouv.fr/en/french-foreign-policy/feminist-diplomacy/the-laboratory-for-women-s-rights-online/. Accessed May 2025.

Law Commission. (2021). *Taking, Making and Sharing Intimate Images Without Consent*. https://lawcom.gov.uk/project/taking-making-and-sharing-intimate-images-without-consent/. Accessed May 2025.

Martin, G. (2019). *Be the change: A toolkit for the activist in you*. Hachette UK.

Massanari, A. (2017). # Gamergate and The Fappening: How Reddit's algorithm, governance, and culture support toxic technocultures. *New Media & Society, 19*(3), 329–346.

Ray, A., & Henry, N. (2025). Sextortion: A scoping review. *Trauma, Violence, & Abuse, 26*(1), 138–155.

The White House. (2023). *White House Task Force to Address Online Harassment and Abuse Blueprint and Final Report*. https://bidenwhitehouse.archives.gov/wp-content/uploads/2024/05/White-House-Task-Force-to-Address-Online-Harassment-and-Abuse_FINAL.pdf. Accessed May 2025.

UK Government. (2015). *Criminal Justice and Courts Act 2015, c. 2, § 33*. https://www.legislation.gov.uk/ukpga/2015/2/section/33. Accessed May 2025.

UK Government. (2019). *Voyeurism (Offences) Act 2019*. https://www.legislation.gov.uk/ukpga/2019/2. Accessed May 2025.

UK Government. (2021). *Domestic Abuse Act 2021: Section 69*. Legislation.gov.uk. https://www.legislation.gov.uk/ukpga/2021/17/section/69/enacted. Accessed May 2025.

UK Government. (2023). *Online Safety Act 2023*. https://www.legislation.gov.uk/ukpga/2023/50. Accessed May 2025.

Umbach, R., Henry, N., Beard, G. F., & Berryessa, C. M. (2024). Non-consensual synthetic intimate imagery: Prevalence, attitudes, and knowledge in 10 countries. In *Proceedings of the 2024 CHI Conference on Human Factors in Computing Systems* (pp. 1–20).

United Nations. (2024). *United Nations Convention against Cybercrime: Strengthening international cooperation for combating certain crimes committed by means of information and communications technology systems and for the sharing of evidence in electronic form of serious crimes* (A/RES/79/243). https://documents.un.org/access.nsf/get?DS=A%2FRES%2F79%2F243&Lang=E. Accessed May 2025.

US Congress. (2025). *TAKE IT DOWN Act, S. 4569, 118th Cong. (2025).* https://www.congress.gov/bill/118th-congress/senate-bill/4569

6

Working Across the Intimate Image Abuse Ecosystem

Abstract This chapter reframes Intimate Image Abuse (IIA) as a systemic issue embedded in a complex, interdependent ecosystem of relationships, institutions, and cultural norms. Drawing on Bronfenbrenner's Ecological Systems Theory and extensive case data from the UK's Revenge Porn Helpline, the chapter illustrates how victims' experiences are shaped not only by perpetrators but also by responses—or failures—at every level of society, including family, law enforcement, workplaces, education, and digital platforms. It exposes how disjointed support systems, poor legal enforcement, underdeveloped public education, and platform inaction exacerbate trauma, while coordinated, victim-centred interventions offer glimpses of what effective response could look like. The analysis further reveals widespread victim-blaming and public misunderstanding about legal protections, especially among young people, due to education systems that focus on risk rather than consent and empowerment. Ultimately, the chapter argues for a whole-systems approach to tackling IIA, calling for cross-sector collaboration, improved education, and institutional accountability to ensure that victims are supported, believed, and protected.

S. Mortimer et al., *Ten Years of the Revenge Porn Helpline*, Palgrave Studies in Victims and Victimology, https://doi.org/10.1007/978-3-032-00614-1_6

Keywords Ecological systems theory · Institutional failure · Victim-blaming culture · Platform accountability · Systemic intervention

Image-based abuse (IBA) is often presented as a problem with a simple origin and a single solution: punish the perpetrator, remove the content, or offer emotional support to the victim. But this linear framing fails to capture the complexity of how such abuse occurs, how it is responded to, and how it is survived. In reality, IBA exists not in isolation but within a wider web of relationships, institutions, and cultural attitudes-an ecosystem of influence, responsibility, and potential failure. We have presented considerable evidence at both an individual and population level to highlight how everyone's experiences are different and there is clearly no simple solution to these issues.

In this chapter, we reframe IBA not as an isolated crime but as a systemic issue that requires an ecosystem approach. We draw on Bronfenbrenner's Ecological Systems Theory (Bronfenbrenner, 1979) to map how individuals affected by IBA are embedded within—and affected by—multiple layers of their social environment: from intimate relationships and family dynamics, to institutional responses from law enforcement and technology companies, to the broader legal, cultural, and educational frameworks that shape public understanding of digital harm. Each of these levels holds the capacity to support or to harm. Crucially, it is the (in)coherence of these systems—their ability or inability to work together—that often determines the outcome for victims.

To ground this theory in practice, we turn to evidence drawn from the UK's Revenge Porn Helpline—an organization that sits at the centre of this ecosystem and engages daily with its failures and possibilities. Using Helpline case data, we examine how victims experience support or abandonment at each level of the ecological system, revealing how fragmented services, cultural stigma, weak legislation, and platform inaction can intensify harm. Just as importantly, we identify examples where coordinated, victim-centred responses show what effective ecosystem-level support can look like.

Ultimately, this chapter is a call to action for a more joined-up approach to IBA: one that recognizes the interdependency of all actors involved and places the needs of victims at the heart of systemic design. Without this shift, interventions will remain partial, reactive, and insufficient. With it, we open the door to meaningful, long-term change.

Ecological Systems Theory

In social and developmental sciences, the term *ecosystem* is used to describe the layered, interconnected contexts in which people live, act, and are acted upon. It is a way of recognizing that no individual is shaped in isolation. Instead, we are embedded in overlapping environments—families, workplaces, schools, legal systems, and media platforms—all of which influence our outcomes.

This ecological perspective is particularly useful when considering systemic failures in victim support. It helps us move beyond the question "what did the victim do?" and towards more urgent questions like:

- What did their community do (or not do)?
- How did institutions respond?
- What legal tools were available and were they usable in practice?
- Is policy and legislation fit for purpose?
- How did cultural norms shape their access to support?

Unlike its biological counterpart the social ecosystem encompasses a network of human relationships, institutions, cultural norms, and systemic structures that collectively influence an individual's development and well-being.

A social ecosystem is not static; it evolves over time and varies across cultures, communities, and individual experiences. It acknowledges that individuals both shape and are shaped by their environments-a principle known as *reciprocal determinism* (Bandura, 1978). For example, a person's behaviour and choices are influenced by their family, school, workplace, and society, but that person can also influence those same systems through their actions, relationships, and responses.

Understanding human experience through an ecological systems-based lens allows for a more holistic approach in disciplines such as psychology, education, social work and public health. It shifts the focus from purely individual traits or behaviours to the broader environments in which individuals are embedded, enabling academics, practitioners and policymakers to identify structural barriers, coordinate interventions, and promote equity across different social systems.

At the core of the theory lies the individual, who is viewed as an active participant within a multilayered ecological context. The most immediate level, the *microsystem*, encompasses the environments in which direct, face-to-face interactions take place. For a child these might include settings such as the family home, classrooms, peer groups, and neighbourhood spaces. The quality and frequency of interactions within these contexts—particularly those involving caregivers, educators, and peers—have a significant and often enduring impact on development. Crucially, the relationships within the microsystem are characterized by bidirectional influence, meaning that the individual both affects and is affected by the surrounding people and settings.

The *mesosystem* refers to the interconnections among the various components of the microsystem. It is within this level that interactions between separate but related environments such as the relationship between home and work take place. The mesosystem emphasizes the developmental importance of consistency and communication across these settings. For instance, in considering child development, the foundations of ecological systems theory, when parents are actively engaged in their child's schooling, there tends to be greater alignment in expectations and support, which can enhance developmental outcomes. Conversely, dissonance or lack of coordination between systems may result in stress or developmental disruption.

The *exosystem* encompasses settings that do not directly involve the individual but nonetheless influence their development through their impact on the microsystem. Examples of such environments include local government agencies, community organizations, and media systems. Although the individual may not be an active participant in these contexts, the events and decisions that occur within them can have significant impacts on the individual's developmental trajectory.

Situated at the broadest level of the model, the *macrosystem* consists of the overarching cultural, economic, legal, and political contexts that shape the values, norms, ideologies, and institutions within a given society. These macro-level forces not only influence the functioning of the other systems but also set the parameters within which development is understood and facilitated. For example, cultural beliefs about childrearing, gender roles, or education inform the structure and expectations embedded in the microsystem and mesosystem. The macrosystem thus serves as the ideological framework that governs the interactions within and between the lower levels of the ecological model.

The final component of Bronfenbrenner's model, the *chronosystem*, introduces the temporal dimension of development. This system accounts for the influence life transitions, as well as historical events, on an individual's outcomes. Temporal changes may be personal (such as parental divorce or relocation) or societal (such as economic recessions or technological shifts). The chronosystem highlights the fact that both the individual and the systems in which they are embedded evolve over time, and that timing and sequencing of events can critically shape developmental pathways.

Collectively, these five interrelated systems offer a systemic understanding of development as a product of continuous interaction between the individual and their environment. Ecological Systems Theory underscores the necessity of contextualizing individual behaviour within broader relational, institutional, and cultural frameworks.

Applications of Ecological Systems Theory in Adult Populations

Although originally developed to explain child development, Bronfenbrenner's Ecological Systems Theory has been widely applied to adult populations across disciplines such as mental health, education, social work, gerontology, and occupational health. Its focus on nested, interacting systems offers a valuable framework for examining the complex environmental influences shaping adult behaviour, well-being, and life outcomes.

In higher education, Donaldson and Graham (1999) used the ecological model to explore how family obligations (microsystem), workplace support (exosystem), and broader institutional norms (macrosystem) affect non-traditional students' persistence and success, highlighting the distinctive challenges adult learners face.

The theory also illuminates the structural roots of adult homelessness. Moxley (2000) identified how individual vulnerabilities, weak service coordination, and systemic policy failures interact across ecological levels, while long-term exclusion and stigma (chronosystem and macrosystem) compound marginalization.

Gerontology applications, such as Lawton and Nahemow's (1973) ecological model of ageing, underscore the dynamic between an individual's capacity and environmental demands. Care networks (microsystem), service accessibility (exosystem), and cultural views on ageing (macrosystem) all influence later-life experiences, especially through transitions like retirement or bereavement (chronosystem).

However, perhaps to most readily applicable to our needs is Heise's work (Heise, 1998) which offers a comprehensive model for understanding the complex roots of violence against women, particularly intimate partner violence. Heise argues that such violence cannot be explained by a single cause or discipline. Instead, it emerges from the interplay of factors operating at multiple levels of a woman's environment—ranging from personal history to broad cultural norms.

Heise highlights how personal experiences and characteristics, such as exposure to violence in childhood, substance abuse, and mental health issues, can increase vulnerability to either perpetrating or experiencing violence. These personal factors are deeply shaped by past trauma and the developmental context of the individual.

Moving outward, the microsystem encompasses a woman's immediate relationships—particularly with intimate partners and family members. Here, dynamics such as power imbalances, relationship conflict, and male dominance play a critical role. Violence is often reinforced in relationships where one partner exerts control over the other, and where emotional or economic dependence limits a woman's ability to leave.

At the exosystem level, Heise examines how broader social structures, such as poverty, social isolation, and the accessibility of support services, either mitigate or exacerbate risk. In communities where violence is normalized, services are underfunded, or women lack access to shelters and legal protection, abuse is more likely to persist.

Finally, the macrosystem includes the wider societal and cultural norms that shape gender roles, power relations, and attitudes towards violence. Patriarchal beliefs, norms that condone male dominance, and a general tolerance for violence all contribute to an environment where abuse is more likely to occur and less likely to be challenged.

Heise's framework is notable because rather than isolating individual or cultural explanations, she emphasizes the interconnectedness of risk factors across different levels. The model not only helps explain why violence occurs, but also points to the need for multi-level prevention strategies—ones that address individual behaviour, relationship dynamics, institutional practices, and societal norms simultaneously. This is a concept immediately applicable to IIA and has been illustrated with discussion from the previous three chapters.

Applying Bronfenbrenner's Ecological Systems Theory to Victims of Intimate Image Abuse

Utilizing Bronfenbrenner's Bioecological Model of Human Development (ibid.) offers a similar comprehensive framework for understanding how different environmental systems shape victims' experiences and determine the effectiveness of the support they receive related to IIA.

At the most immediate level, the *microsystem* comprises the direct interpersonal relationships and environments that immediately influence the victim's well-being. This includes family members, close friends, healthcare providers, legal representatives, and frontline law enforcement officers. Victims benefit significantly from non-judgmental emotional support provided by family and peers, which can counteract the acute feelings of shame, isolation, and distress commonly associated with image-based abuse. Immediate engagement with police and victim support organizations can offer both protection and guidance, including assistance with image removal and reporting mechanisms.

However, challenges at the microsystem level are common, as we will explore below. Victims may encounter blame or scepticism from family members or experience social stigma among their peers. Furthermore, limited access to affordable and specialized mental health services may delay recovery and contribute to long-term psychological consequences.

The *mesosystem* refers to the interplay between the various components of the microsystem. In the context of image-based abuse, this includes how different support networks-such as family members, mental health professionals, legal advocates, and educational institutions-interact with one another. Effective interventions at this level involve coordinated efforts among these groups. For example, partnerships between law enforcement agencies, technology companies and support services can facilitate the rapid takedown of non-consensual images (as we have discussed in earlier chapters around StopNCII.org).

The *exosystem* encompasses broader social structures and institutional policies that indirectly influence victims, even when there is no direct interaction. Technology companies, for instance, play a crucial role in moderating and removing explicit content, providing the tools for reporting and developing detection tools can significantly reduce the circulation of abusive material. Workplaces also have a responsibility to develop policies that protect and support employees who are targeted, including confidential reporting mechanisms and access to psychological support.

Media organizations and advocacy groups contribute to public awareness campaigns aimed at promoting consent, digital safety, and destigmatization. Additionally, legislative reforms are a vital component of exosystem-level intervention. Enhancements to revenge porn laws—such as improved prosecution mechanisms, higher penalties for offenders, and better victim protections—serve as systemic deterrents.

Nevertheless, several structural challenges persist. As we have discussed, legislative processes can be slow to adapt to emerging forms of digital harm, leaving victims vulnerable and without timely legal recourse. Technology companies may hesitate to assume full responsibility for content regulation, citing free speech concerns or technical limitations. Similarly, many workplaces (see below) remain unprepared to support employees facing such forms of abuse, resulting in inadequate protection and secondary victimization.

The *macrosystem* comprises the dominant cultural values, societal attitudes, and ideological frameworks that shape all other layers of the ecological model. In the context of revenge pornography, cultural narratives often perpetuate victim-blaming, gender stereotypes, and misunderstandings about consent, all of which contribute to the stigmatization of victims and discourage help-seeking behaviour. Media portrayals that sensationalize cases of image-based abuse can exacerbate trauma and create additional barriers to reporting.

Efforts to shift public discourse are therefore crucial. Public education campaigns aimed at reframing narratives around digital consent and sexual autonomy can challenge harmful norms. Integrating digital consent education into comprehensive sex education curricula is particularly important in equipping young people with the knowledge and tools to navigate online spaces safely.

Finally, the *chronosystem* captures the role of time in shaping both individual experiences and systemic responses to image-based abuse. Historically, IIA was not widely recognized as a criminal offence, and victims often had no legal recourse. Cultural silence and stigma further compounded the harm by isolating victims and deterring disclosure.

In recent years, as we have discussed in previous chapters, significant progress has been made. Technological advancements (discussed in more detail in the next chapter) offer new possibilities for timely intervention. Legal reforms now place a duty of care on tech platforms to protect users from harmful content, and NCII is a *priority offence*. These are, in the eyes of the legislator, the most serious and prevalent illegal content and activity online, requiring platforms to take proactive measures to prevent users from encountering them. Concurrently, cultural narratives around consent, digital ethics, and online privacy are evolving, contributing to greater awareness and prevention efforts.

By viewing victims within the context of their ecological environments, this model encourages a shift away from individualized blame and towards structural accountability, emphasizing the interdependence of

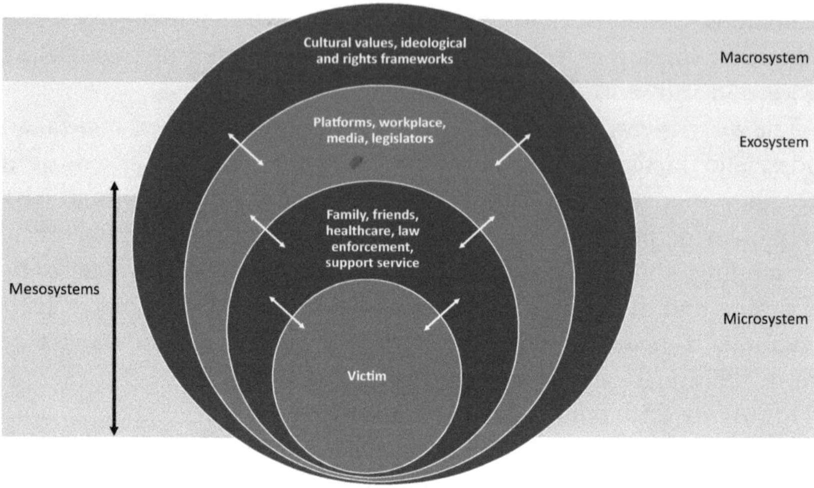

Fig. 6.1 An Ecosystem View of Intimate Image Abuse

legal, social, psychological, and technological systems in the prevention and redress of image-based sexual abuse (Fig. 6.1).

In the second half of this chapter, we return to the case data from the Helpline to further explore the roles of stakeholders against the ecological model to better understand where the system breaks down and how these issues might be addressed. We return to themes discussed in previous chapters, reinforcing themes and illustrating them against an ecosystem model.

The People Around the Victim: How Stakeholders Influence the Experience of Image-Based Abuse

Image-based abuse impacts multiple areas of a victim's life, including personal relationships, workplaces, legal processes, and online activity. Data from Helpline case logs indicate the involvement of a broad network of individuals and institutions—such as family members, friends, former partners, law enforcement, employers, and digital platforms—that influence victims' experiences in various ways. These actors may provide support or contribute to challenges in addressing the abuse. While we have explored some of these dimensions (for example, abusive partners or law enforcement response) in previous chapters, we will reiterate some of these perspectives here against the ecosystem model.

Ex-Partners: The Most Common Perpetrators

Perhaps an unsurprising finding, but one worth reiterating, from the analysis is that a significant number of cases involve ex-partners. For many victims, the person who once held their trust and intimacy becomes their abuser, using private images as a weapon of humiliation, control, or revenge.

Some victims describe how an ex leaked their images publicly, seeking to ruin their reputation after a breakup. Others tell of being threatened repeatedly, their abuser dangling the possibility of exposure as leverage to force them into compliance—whether that means staying in a relationship, sending more explicit content, or fulfilling other demands.

This betrayal leaves victims not just dealing with the violation itself, but also with the emotional devastation of having their trust shattered. Many express regret, self-blame, and a sense of powerlessness, knowing that someone they once loved and trusted is now orchestrating their humiliation.

Friends and Family: Supportive or Judgemental?

The disclosures reveal that family relationships are often deeply entwined in the trauma of IIA. For many victims, family is not just a source of support—it is also a source of fear, shame, and emotional vulnerability. A recurring pattern in the accounts is that perpetrators frequently threaten to send explicit images or videos to victims' family members. This includes parents, siblings, children, and even extended family. The intent behind these threats is to exploit the victim's emotional ties and sense of responsibility, especially within families where reputation and honour are deeply valued.

These threats are highly effective because many victims live in fear of being judged or rejected by their families. Several describe feeling overwhelmed by the idea that their loved ones might find out what has happened. There is a strong undercurrent of anticipated shame in these disclosures. Victims worry about how they'll be perceived—whether they'll be blamed for what occurred, misunderstood, or even abandoned.

In some cases, these fears are unfortunately realized. One victim from a strict religious background was completely cut off by her family after her ex-partner shared intimate content with them. Her husband divorced her, and her relatives stopped speaking to her. This kind of rejection is not isolated—it appears elsewhere in the data as well, particularly where family values or social expectations are deeply conservative. In such instances, the abuse becomes compounded by the emotional trauma of familial abandonment.

However, not all experiences are negative. Some victims describe family members, particularly parents or partners, who encouraged them to seek help, supported them emotionally, or even acted on their behalf. In a few cases, concerned friends or relatives made the initial contact with support services, recognizing that the victim was too distressed to do so themselves. These examples demonstrate the powerful role that family can play in helping victims recover and seek justice, especially when they respond with compassion and understanding.

It is also important to note that some victims are parents themselves. A few, including victims who were pregnant at the time of the abuse or had young children, expressed fears not just for their own reputations but also for how the situation might affect their children. One expressed significant concern that her intimate images might be leaked just weeks before giving birth. For these victims, the abuse threatens not only their privacy and safety, but also their role as caregivers and protectors.

Despite the presence of supportive families in some accounts, many victims choose not to disclose the abuse to their loved ones at all. This silence often stems from fear-fear of being shamed, disbelieved, or hurting those they care about. Cultural taboos, generational gaps, and misunderstandings about online abuse further compound this reluctance to speak. In this way, family becomes both central to the experience of the abuse and yet often absent from the victim's support system.

In summary, the role of family in these disclosures is complex and deeply emotional. Family members are frequently used by abusers to intimidate and control. Victims often fear judgment and stigma, and in some cases, those fears come true. At the same time, there are examples where family support is present and invaluable. The disclosures make it clear that family can be either a source of profound distress or a critical lifeline and sometimes both.

Law Enforcement Responses to Image-Based Abuse: A System Failing Victims

We have already discussed in Chapters 4 and 5 how some victims of IIA have experienced negative responses from law enforcement and the criminal justice system. We can draw further examples here to reiterate this point from the perspective of law enforcement being a part of the ecosystem. The analysis paints a troubling picture of how law enforcement professionals respond to cases of image-based abuse, including sextortion, revenge porn, coercion, and online blackmail. While some victims encounter officers who are supportive and proactive, many report frustration, dismissal, and legal loopholes that prevent them from obtaining justice. The response of police forces and legal systems to these crimes is inconsistent, bureaucratically slow, and, in many cases, ineffective, leaving victims feeling abandoned by the institutions meant to protect them.

One of the most persistent issues is the reluctance or inability of law enforcement to take these cases seriously. Many victims describe experiences where police officers dismissed their reports outright, often failing to recognize the seriousness of the crime. A recurring response from authorities is that because victims originally shared the images voluntarily, the case is considered a personal mistake rather than a criminal act, something that is not true and reflects a victim-blaming mentality among some law enforcement professionals. Even in cases where offenders explicitly threaten to release images unless demands are met, some victims are told that until the images are leaked, no crime has been committed. Again, this is not true.

One victim, whose ex-partner repeatedly threatened to expose intimate photos unless she complied with his demands, was told by police that since she had originally consented to taking the images, the threats did not qualify as a criminal act. In another case, a victim reported ongoing blackmail by a stranger who had obtained her private images, only to be told that there was nothing the police could do unless the images had already been shared online. These responses force victims into a waiting game of emotional distress, knowing that they may have to endure actual exposure and humiliation before authorities are willing to intervene.

The dataset also highlights stark inconsistencies in law enforcement responses and also the international dimension on inquiries the helpline receives. In countries such as the UK, USA, Canada, and parts of Europe, revenge porn laws and sextortion legislation have improved in recent years, but police enforcement, it seems from the data, remains inconsistent. Some victims describe interacting with well-trained officers who understood the nuances of digital abuse, while others found themselves speaking to officers unfamiliar with the laws, leading to misinformation or refusal to act.

In many non-Western countries, the legal framework for image-based abuse is weak or non-existent, leaving victims with little to no recourse. Some women in conservative societies reported that they feared reporting the crime would backfire not only would their complaint be dismissed, but they might face legal punishment themselves for being in an intimate image in the first place. In one case, a woman hesitated to involve the police because morality laws in her country criminalized nudity, and she feared being arrested rather than protected.

Another major obstacle for victims is law enforcement's inability to deal with cross-border cases. Many sextortion scams originate from organized criminal gangs operating overseas, particularly in Nigeria, the Philippines, and parts of Eastern Europe. Victims who reach out to police often receive the same response: because the perpetrator is outside their jurisdiction, there is little they can do.

One victim, blackmailed into paying over £2,000 to an extortionist based in another country, was told by authorities that tracking and prosecuting the offender was impossible. Another victim, who had clear evidence of blackmail, was informed that police could not act because the perpetrator was using a VPN and a fake account. These cases highlight a critical gap in international law enforcement cooperation, which criminals are aware of and exploit freely.

Even in cases where authorities are willing to help, victims often face long delays and bureaucratic barriers. Many victims describe their cases as being slowly processed over months or even years, with no clear updates on progress. Police often lack the resources or expertise to track down and remove explicit content, leaving victims to navigate the complex and often ineffective content takedown process on their own.

One woman, who had been trying to remove images of herself from the internet for over a decade, explained how she had issued *thousands* of DMCA notices to different websites-yet new uploads kept appearing. Law enforcement provided little assistance beyond legal advice, leaving her to continue an exhausting and emotionally draining battle on her own. The slowness of police responses means that offenders often have ample time to continue their abuse, re-uploading content to new platforms faster than victims can have it removed.

As we have discussed previously (and previously published—Bond and Tyrrell [2021]) lack of specialized training among police officers also contributes to inconsistent and ineffective responses. Victims frequently describe interactions with officers who seemed unfamiliar with image-based abuse laws, leading to misinformation about legal options and next steps. Some officers were unaware of how to request content removal from major social media platforms, leaving victims to figure out the reporting process on their own.

One victim, after reporting a blackmail case to law enforcement, was incorrectly told there were no laws protecting her, despite existing revenge porn legislation that applied directly to her case. It was only after seeking legal advice from an advocacy group that she was able to push the police to take her complaint seriously. This lack of consistent and comprehensive training means that some victims receive meaningful help while others are left completely unsupported, depending entirely on the knowledge level of the specific officers they speak to.

Perhaps the most disturbing theme in the dataset is the victim-blaming attitude displayed by some law enforcement professionals. Instead of treating victims as survivors of abuse, some officers shame or ridicule them, implying that they are responsible for their own victimization.

A victim who was blackmailed after exchanging intimate images was laughed at by police when he tried to report his case, leaving him feeling humiliated and unwilling to seek further help. Another whose intimate images were leaked by an ex-partner was told she should "be more careful in the future" rather than given meaningful legal assistance. These responses reinforce harmful social stigmas, discouraging victims from reporting their cases or seeking help.

The analysis makes it clear that law enforcement's response to image-based abuse is deeply flawed. Victims face dismissal, jurisdictional challenges, long delays, lack of specialized training among officers, and even outright victim-blaming, making it extremely difficult for them to get justice. Even in cases where laws exist to protect them, poor enforcement and bureaucratic inefficiencies often render those protections meaningless.

Frustratingly over the lifetime of the Helpline this is a consistent finding—offenders will continue to exploit legal gaps, and victims will remain largely unprotected. Image-based abuse is a deeply invasive and psychologically damaging crime, and law enforcement's failure to address it effectively is leaving countless victims without the justice and support they deserve.

Workplaces and Schools: Fear of Professional Consequences

The set of disclosures by victims of image-based abuse reveals much about their perceptions of how employers might respond to such situations, even though direct references to employers are rare. What emerges instead is a clear pattern of fear, silence, and mistrust—suggesting that victims largely view employers as potential risks rather than sources of support.

Many victims express intense anxiety about the possibility of their explicit images or videos being shared with colleagues or professional networks. Platforms like LinkedIn are mentioned in threats made by perpetrators, which implies that victims believe the exposure of such content could jeopardize their jobs or damage their professional reputations. This fear is often so pronounced that some victims mention it as a greater concern than the abuse itself. It reflects a belief that employers might judge them harshly, even when they are clearly the victims of a crime.

A striking theme throughout the disclosures is the absence of employer support. Victims often mention reaching out to friends, family, police, support organizations or online platforms for help but not their employers. This lack of mention suggests that victims do not feel safe disclosing their situations at work, either due to shame or fear of repercussions.

Further, some victims worry that merely reporting the abuse to the police may harm them professionally. For instance, one victim was concerned that his report of being sextorted would appear in a background check for a new job. This highlights the fear that being associated with any kind of intimate image abuse, even as a victim, might carry stigma in the eyes of employers.

The fact that perpetrators often threaten to send content directly to victims' workplaces also reveals something critical: they know that this tactic is effective. They rely on the perceived reputational damage such an act could cause. It's clear that, in the minds of many victims, employers are seen as more likely to penalize or distance themselves from someone involved in an IIA case than to offer support.

Overall, while employers are rarely mentioned directly, these disclosures paint a concerning picture of workplace attitudes. Victims seem to assume that employers lack the policies, awareness, or empathy needed to respond constructively. As a result, they suffer in silence, fearing judgement, job loss, or damage to their careers.

In essence, these accounts suggest that employers are currently seen not as allies in the fight against image-based abuse, but as potential threats to victims' stability and dignity in the aftermath.

The Role of Technology Platforms in Intimate Image Abuse

For many victims of image-based abuse, social media platforms are both the host of the images used to abuse and their, as it is perceived, only form of defence. These platforms are often where abusers first obtain and distribute intimate images, but they are also the first-place victims turn to in order to regain control over their privacy. The analysis reveals a frustrating and largely ineffective response from these platforms, with victims struggling to have their images removed, encountering automated and impersonal responses, and facing long delays with little or no resolution.

One of the most common actions taken by victims is to report the abusive content, hoping that the platform will immediately take it down and ban the perpetrator. However, many describe submitting report after report with no response or action, feeling as though their complaints are being ignored by an automated system. Others detail an exhausting cycle where they report an image, see it removed, only for it to resurface elsewhere a few days later. Instead of solving the problem, social media's slow and inconsistent enforcement forces victims into a relentless game of whack-a-mole, constantly monitoring platforms and repeating the reporting process over and over.

Even when content is successfully removed, victims often find the process slow, allowing the damage to spread before any action is taken. Some describe waiting weeks or even months for a response, only to be met with a generic automated reply stating that their complaint does not violate platform policies. The lack of urgency in these responses leaves victims frustrated and vulnerable, knowing that the longer their images remain online, the more people will see them, share them, or use them for further blackmail.

For those facing ongoing harassment or repeated leaks, the situation becomes even more dire. Victims who have their images repeatedly uploaded across different accounts or platforms express anger and exhaustion at having to fight the same battle repeatedly. Some describe contacting social media companies directly, only to receive no meaningful assistance. They are told to report the content through standard channels, despite already doing so multiple times, or worse—they receive no response at all.

A major frustration expressed by victims is that social media platforms claim to have strict policies against non-consensual content yet fail to enforce them effectively. Some victims mention cases where perpetrators manipulate the images slightly cropping them, blurring faces, or posting them in a private group-to bypass detection algorithms, allowing the abuse to continue unchecked. In other cases, platforms reject takedown requests, claiming the images do not explicitly violate their guidelines, despite clear evidence that they were shared without consent.

Beyond content removal, victims also expect platforms to act against the abusers themselves, yet this rarely happens. Banning perpetrators is the exception, not the rule, with many victims frustrated by how easily abusers can create new accounts and continue their harassment. Even in cases where offenders are repeatedly reported for the same behaviour, victims report that platforms take no decisive action to prevent them from targeting new people. Meanwhile, some victims have had their own accounts suspended for making too many reports, an irony that punishes those trying to protect themselves while allowing abusers to remain active.

These frustrations with platforms extend beyond mainstream platforms. While Facebook, Instagram, and Twitter are frequently mentioned, many victims also struggle to remove content from adult websites and private messaging platforms like Telegram, WhatsApp, and Reddit. On these sites, the process of reporting abuse is even less transparent, with little accountability and even fewer guarantees of content removal. Some adult platforms require legal documentation or proof of identity before taking down stolen content, placing the burden on the victim to constantly prove their victimhood to reclaim their privacy. Others simply ignore requests unless multiple complaints are filed, making the takedown process an uphill battle that few have the energy to fight indefinitely.

For victims, the lack of action from social media platforms and online services can be devastating. Many describe feeling helpless, exhausted, and abandoned, knowing that the platforms that helped spread their violation are doing little to help them reclaim their dignity. The reality is that these companies, despite having the resources to respond swiftly, often fail to prioritize the safety of their users, instead choosing to implement slow, bureaucratic processes that delay justice and prolong victim suffering.

Support Services: A Last Resort, but Often Underutilized

While there are references to counsellors, helplines, and advocacy groups, the analysis suggests that many victims do not access professional support services and will turn to the Helpline online in the last resort.

Some may simply not be aware of available help, while others may not feel safe discussing their trauma with strangers. The relatively low mention of mental health professionals highlights a serious gap in victim recovery, as many are left to process their experiences alone, without the psychological support they need.

This raises a crucial question: If victims are turning first to family, friends, and the legal system—often with disappointing results—who is truly supporting them in the long run? The absence of structured emotional support in many cases suggests that victims of image-based abuse are often left to struggle in silence.

The analysis makes it clear that victims of image-based abuse do not navigate their trauma alone but not all of those around them are allies.

- Ex-partners are the most common perpetrators, weaponizing private images for revenge, coercion, or humiliation.
- Friends and family provide mixed reactions, sometimes offering support, but often reinforcing shame and blame.

- Law enforcement fails many victims, leaving them without legal recourse.
- Workplaces and universities add another layer of fear, making exposure not just a personal crisis, but a professional threat.
- Social media platforms have immense power to protect victims but often fail to act swiftly or effectively.
- Support services remain underutilized, leaving victims without adequate mental health care.

Image-based abuse is not just a crime against an individual—it is a social issue that plays out across families, institutions, and online spaces. The response of those around the victim can either help them recover or deepen their trauma, making these stakeholders a crucial part of both the problem and the solution.

The analysis shows clear evidence of the essential role the Revenge Porn Helpline plays in supporting victims of image-based abuse. For many, it is not just a resource—it is the first and often only place they turn for help. The cases reveal how victims rely on the Helpline for guidance on removing images, legal advice, and emotional support, though some areas of its service remain underutilized or less widely known.

One of the most striking insights is that victims frequently contact the Helpline without knowing what to do next. Many of those reaching out express uncertainty, distress, and a need for reassurance, using phrases that suggest they are seeking clarity on their options. The Helpline becomes a crucial first point of contact, giving them the knowledge and confidence to act. Whether they are reporting an incident for the first time, trying to navigate a confusing legal system, or simply looking for someone to listen, the Helpline fills a gap left by other institutions, such as law enforcement and social media platforms.

One of the most valued aspects of the service is its support for content removal. Many victims struggle with getting social media platforms, adult websites, or messaging apps to take down non-consensual images, often encountering delays, ignored reports, or bureaucratic obstacles. The Helpline appears to play a key role in assisting victims through this process, either by submitting reports on their behalf, guiding them through platform policies, or escalating their complaints when they are being ignored. This assistance is especially crucial in cases where images keep resurfacing on different sites, creating an ongoing cycle of distress for victims.

Beyond content removal, legal support is another critical area of need, though the dataset suggests that this aspect of the Helpline's services may be more limited. Some victims explicitly seek legal advice, mentioning concerns about court proceedings, restraining orders, or prosecution. However, legal support is referenced far less frequently than content removal, suggesting that the Helpline may not provide direct legal representation but instead offers general guidance or referrals to external services. This could point to a larger issue—victims may be looking for stronger legal protections that the Helpline is unable to provide, highlighting a gap in accessible legal support for image-based abuse cases.

Interestingly, while emotional support is available, it seems to be less commonly sought out by victims. There are some references to seeking reassurance, counselling, or psychological support, but far fewer than mentions of help with practical matters like image takedowns. This raises an important question: Do victims know that emotional support is available, or do they feel hesitant to ask for it? It is possible that many focus on resolving the immediate crisis—getting their images taken down—before considering the longer-term emotional impact.

One theme remains consistent throughout the analysis: victims trust the Helpline. There is a strong sense of relief and gratitude in the way many describe reaching out, suggesting that they feel heard, taken seriously, and supported in a way that they do not experience elsewhere. Many victims have already faced dismissal by social media platforms, frustration with law enforcement, and judgment from family or friends-yet the Helpline stands out as a place where they can finally get real help.

The data reveals the Revenge Porn Helpline as a vital and effective service, particularly in helping victims regain control over their images and navigating digital platforms. However, there are opportunities for further expansion and outreach, particularly in promoting emotional support services and strengthening legal assistance options. By continuing to adapt to victims' needs and advocating for better protections and faster responses from tech companies, the Helpline can remain a trusted and invaluable resource for those affected by image-based abuse.

Understanding Victim Knowledge and Education Around Image-Based Abuse

The Helpline enquiry data offers important insights into how victims of image-based abuse perceive and understand the law, their rights, and the support systems available to them. In exploring ecosystem response to IIA, this is an extremely useful piece of analysis to highlight flaws in the macrosystem. While we have, through this book, shown that legislation to support victims of IIA is improving, this is not the only role of the macrosystem. Education policy is a crucial part of the ecosystem when exploring holistic responses to IIA. An informed population who understands this abuse, that it is not acceptable, how the paths available to them to challenge this abuse, will be far stronger than one that does not believe they deserve to get help and support.

In exploring this vital aspect of the ecosystem, through analysis of case disclosures, we can, in turn, unpick the quality of public and school-based education around IIA. What emerges from the analysis is a consistent pattern of uncertainty, misinformation, and in many cases, complete unfamiliarity with legal protections and available resources. These knowledge gaps reflect broader societal shortcomings in how image-based abuse is communicated and addressed through public education and institutional systems.

One of the most prominent themes in the data is the widespread confusion around what constitutes a criminal offence. Victims frequently question whether the behaviour they are experiencing falls under the legal definitions of image-based abuse. For instance, individuals are unsure whether sharing a previously consensual image without permission is illegal, or whether content posted to subscription platforms like OnlyFans is protected under existing intimate image laws. Others question whether they can act if the image was taken without their knowledge, or if the content in question is AI-generated or altered, as in cases of deepfakes. This uncertainty is not a reflection of ignorance on the part of victims, but of the legal system's failure to provide accessible, public-facing information that reflects the realities of contemporary digital life.

Closely linked to this is the limited awareness of reporting pathways and victim support services. Many victims arrive at the Helpline only after exhausting other routes, often having been turned away by the police or referred by a friend or institution. Very few appear to be aware, prior to contact, of digital tools such as StopNCII.org, or of their right to report content under laws related to intimate image abuse. This reactive engagement with support systems suggests that public information about these services is not widely visible or embedded in everyday digital spaces. As a result, many victims delay seeking help, or do not seek help at all, until the harm has escalated.

In addition to legal uncertainty, the data shows that victims often do not understand how to document or preserve evidence of abuse. Several messages indicate confusion about whether screenshots, links, or anonymous messages are sufficient to prove that abuse occurred. In some cases, victims express anxiety that the evidence has already been deleted or is difficult to trace, leading to feelings of helplessness and a belief that nothing can be done. Others indicate they were not informed by the police or any other body on how to submit evidence, or what to expect from the legal process if they did pursue a complaint. This points to a broader lack of education not only around legal rights, but around practical digital literacy and evidence-handling in cases of online harm.

Stigma and shame also play a powerful role in limiting victim knowledge. Some individuals express guilt for having sent intimate images in the first place, or fear that reporting the incident will lead to further victimization—whether through judgment, disbelief, or reputational damage. This is particularly common among younger victims and those from marginalized communities, who may feel that they will not be taken seriously or may be blamed for their own victimization. The presence of internalized shame in these accounts suggests that existing public education does not do enough to challenge harmful narratives around sexuality, digital consent, and image sharing. Rather than framing consensual image exchange as a normal aspect of digital relationships, dominant narratives continue to treat it as reckless or irresponsible behaviour thus deterring victims from recognizing the abuse they've experienced and seeking support.

There is also clear evidence in the analysis of confusion around jurisdiction and platform accountability. Victims often report cases involving perpetrators based overseas, such as in sextortion scams. In these cases, they are frequently told that nothing can be done, or that law enforcement does not have the means to pursue an international investigation. Others express frustration that content remains online despite repeated requests to platforms for its removal. This confusion highlights the lack of public guidance around the responsibilities of digital platforms, how global content moderation works, and what legal mechanisms exist—or don't exist—for transnational enforcement of intimate image abuse laws.

Taken together, these insights point to a significant deficit in public education around image-based abuse. More comprehensive, accessible, and inclusive education is needed, not only for young people in schools, but across all levels of society. This includes education on:

- The legal definitions and boundaries of consent and image-based abuse.
- How and where to report content, and what the process will involve.
- How to collect and store evidence securely.
- The distinction between consensual image-sharing and non-consensual distribution.
- How to access victim services, removal tools, and privacy-preserving technologies.

Such education should be embedded in multiple contexts, from digital literacy curricula and sexual education programmes in schools, to onboarding resources in workplaces, university induction sessions, and even guidance integrated into social media platforms and dating apps. Crucially, this education must also be designed to affirm the rights of individuals to express themselves digitally without fear of abuse or shame. It must explicitly reject victim-blaming narratives and recognize that the harm lies not in the act of sharing an intimate image, but in the betrayal of consent and privacy that occurs when that image is misused.

Does the Helpline Data Show Evidence of Victim-Blaming?

The Helpline data reveals a troubling and consistent pattern: many victims of image-based abuse internalize blame for the harm they have suffered. This self-blame often stems from a cultural and educational environment that focuses on risk and responsibility, rather than consent and accountability. The result is a landscape in which victims frequently feel ashamed, embarrassed, and responsible not just for their actions, but for the abuse inflicted upon them.

Several of the messages contain explicit statements of self-directed blame. In one particularly striking case, a young man reflects on his experience of being lured into sharing intimate images online. "I hate myself for becoming this obsessed with love", he writes, describing how his emotional vulnerability led him to trust someone who later exploited him. He goes on to chastise himself and say that he knows that it is his fault. There is little sense in the message that the person who misused his trust bears responsibility.

This sense of blame is echoed in other messages. One victim, reflecting on how she was blackmailed after sharing an image, simply stated that she knows it is her fault for sending images to a stranger. The tone is resigned, and the implication is clear-by sharing the image, she feels she has forfeited any claim to protection. This narrative, where sending an image equates to accepting the risk of abuse, mirrors the messaging often embedded in school-based sexting education: don't send the image, and you won't be harmed. What's missing is an emphasis on the role of the perpetrator and the violation of consent.

In many cases, this internalized blame is accompanied by feelings of intense shame, saying they have been stupid for falling for the scam. Another felt pressured into sending images but when they did say that they were stupid for doing so. This suggests not only regret but a belief that the victim's own decisions, rather than the abuser's threats and manipulation, are the true cause of harm.

These emotional responses are not isolated. One victim, also targeted through an online sextortion scam, concluded that they would never look for affection online again and that they knew technically it was their own fault for sending images. Here, the individual attributes their victimization not just to their actions but to their desires-to seek connection, to trust someone, to explore intimacy online. These are basic human impulses, yet in the absence of affirming education and societal support, they become a source of shame and moral self-judgment.

Collectively, these examples demonstrate how poorly equipped many victims are to interpret their experiences through a lens of rights and consent, rather than one of risk and responsibility. Current approaches to education around sexting and image-based abuse often focus heavily on legality—what not to do, and what laws may be broken. While understanding the legal consequences is important, this emphasis can leave young people with the impression that the mere act of sending an image negates their right to protection if it is later shared without consent.

Worse still, such framing can actively discourage disclosure and help-seeking. If victims believe they are to blame-or fear that others will blame them—they may choose to stay silent. The emotional cost of shame, combined with the fear of judgment from parents, peers, police, or educators, becomes a barrier to support. This is particularly concerning when many of these cases involve manipulation, coercion, or grooming-forms of abuse that are unlikely to be recognized or named if the primary narrative is one of personal responsibility.

The cases from this dataset are illustrative of a wider educational and cultural failure. They show the urgent need for relationships and sex education that does not merely warn against risk but affirms young people's rights to bodily autonomy, digital consent, and emotional safety. Victims must be taught that consent can be withdrawn, that trust does not imply fault, and that abuse is never justified by the actions of the person targeted. Without this shift, we risk perpetuating cycles of silence, shame, and self-blame that continue to isolate those most in need of care.

In short, the Helpline data makes clear that there is an urgent need to strengthen public understanding of image-based abuse not just by improving the law, but by ensuring that people know how to navigate it. Without clear, compassionate, and accessible education, even the most robust legal or technical tools will remain out of reach for many victims. Addressing this gap is a critical part of building a more responsive and supportive system for those affected by intimate image abuse.

However, if we are to explore current provision around education in England, where the Helpline receives most of its enquiries, we can see that this is lacking.

In England, the national curriculum mandates that all secondary schools provide Relationships and Sex Education (RSE).[1] The focus of image-based abuse in this education centres including the legal and ethical considerations surrounding online behaviours such as sexting and the non-consensual sharing of images.

- **Legal Awareness**: Students are educated about the legal implications of sharing personal information, pictures, videos, and other material using technology. This includes understanding what is lawful and unlawful, thereby helping students discern right from wrong in the context of online interactions.
- **Online Behaviour**: The curriculum addresses online behaviours, emphasizing the importance of respectful and responsible use of technology. Topics such as image and information sharing, commonly referred to as "sexting", are discussed to highlight potential risks and consequences.
- **Safeguarding Issues**: Students learn about broader safeguarding concerns, including the non-consensual sharing of private sexual images or videos. They are informed that such actions are illegal and can lead to serious legal consequences.

The curriculum also underscores the importance of understanding consent, the age of consent, and the significance of healthy relationships. By integrating these topics, the RSE curriculum aims to provide students with a comprehensive understanding of the complexities and responsibilities associated with relationships and sexual activity in the digital age.

However, the focus of this education remains on simple messages of "this is illegal" and, as explored in other research (Phippen, 2016, 2025) could be argued underpins victim-blaming narratives. While the

[1] https://www.gov.uk/government/publications/relationships-education-relationships-and-sex-education-rse-and-health-education. Accessed May 2025.

national Relationships and Sex Education (RSE) curriculum in England does incorporate important legal guidance around image-based abuse and sexting, there are valid concerns that its framing may place too much emphasis on legality and in doing so, may risk reinforcing victim-blaming narratives or failing to fully meet the emotional and social needs of young people.

The curriculum clearly states that pupils should be taught about the legal consequences of non-consensual image sharing, including the criminalization of sharing sexual images without consent and the possession or distribution of indecent images of children—even when self-generated. While legal awareness is undeniably important, especially in deterring harmful behaviour and empowering young people to recognize abuse, the predominant emphasis on legal risk can be problematic.

In many schools, this legal framing often becomes the dominant message: "*Don't sext-it's illegal*". This can lead to an overly simplistic, punitive approach that fails to acknowledge why young people engage in consensual image sharing in the first place—whether as part of developing sexual identities, exploring intimacy, or responding to social pressures. Without this context, the conversation can easily shift from one about consent, respect, and digital boundaries to one that focuses on avoidance and fear, which may inadvertently discourage victims from seeking help when something goes wrong.

When sexting is framed solely as a risky or unlawful behaviour, victims of image-based abuse may be made to feel complicit in their own harm. If students are repeatedly told not to share images "because they might be leaked", the implication is that those who do are to blame when abuse occurs. This logic mirrors wider societal victim-blaming tropes, such as those seen in cases of sexual assault: that the victim should have known better, acted differently, or avoided placing themselves in a vulnerable position.

This framing can be especially damaging for young people who have experienced coercion, grooming, or blackmail-contexts in which the image sharing may not have been freely chosen, even if not overtly forced. It can also silence victims who feel ashamed or fear punishment from parents, teachers, or the law itself. When the focus is on rule-breaking rather than care, victims may be less likely to disclose harm or seek support.

Finally, it's important to note that while the curriculum outlines key content, implementation varies widely across schools. Some institutions deliver RSE through comprehensive, inclusive, and well-trained approaches; others offer minimal coverage or rely on outdated, moralistic narratives. Teachers themselves often report feeling underprepared to tackle subjects like sexting or image-based abuse, especially where the legal implications are complex or emotionally charged and there might be resistance from other stakeholders (for example, see Cumper et al., 2024).

In short, while the RSE curriculum rightly includes education around the legal aspects of image-based abuse and sexting, it can risk becoming overly legalistic and insufficiently empathetic. This emphasis may unintentionally reinforce victim-blaming messages, overlook the broader social and emotional dimensions of abuse, and create barriers for disclosure and support.

To address this, RSE needs to move beyond a framework of "risk and responsibility" and towards one rooted in care, consent, and digital empowerment-helping young people not just avoid harm, but understand their rights, navigate relationships safely, and seek support without shame if things go wrong.

Conclusions

Intimate image abuse (IIA) cannot be adequately understood or addressed through the lens of any single system, institution, or actor. As this chapter has demonstrated, it is a deeply embedded social harm, shaped and sustained by the interplay of personal relationships, institutional responses, cultural norms, and technological infrastructures. Using an ecological systems framework, we have examined how each layer—from the individual and their immediate relationships, to global tech platforms and international law—contributes to either mitigating or compounding the trauma of IIA.

Victims do not suffer in a vacuum; their experiences are profoundly affected by how those around them respond. When family members offer support, workplaces enact protective policies, law enforcement takes complaints seriously, and platforms act quickly to remove abusive content, victims can begin to reclaim control and recover. But when these same actors dismiss, delay, or blame, the harm deepens. What emerges from the Helpline's case data is a stark picture of a system that is, at times, fragmented, reactive, and unprepared. Too often, victims are left to navigate abuse alone, through a maze of inconsistent services and uncoordinated responses.

This chapter calls for a shift in our collective understanding of IIA—from seeing it as an individual problem to recognizing it as a systemic failure that requires a systemic response. It demands that all stakeholders-families, educators, police, legislators, employers, platforms, and support services-begin to see themselves not as isolated actors, but as interconnected parts of a larger, shared responsibility. No one system or organization can fix this alone, but together, with coordination and purpose, we can begin to build an ecosystem that truly protects, supports, and empowers those most at risk.

References

Bandura, A. (1978). The self system in reciprocal determinism. *American Psychologist, 33*(4), 344.

Bond, E., & Tyrrell, K. (2021). Understanding revenge pornography: A national survey of police officers and staff in England and Wales. *Journal of Interpersonal Violence, 36*(5–6), 2166–2181.

Bronfenbrenner, U. (1979). *The ecology of human development: Experiments by nature and design.* Harvard University Press.

Cumper, P., Adams, S., Onyejekwe, K., & O'Reilly, M. (2024). Teachers' perspectives on relationships and sex education lessons in England. *Sex Education, 24*(2), 238–254.

Donaldson, J. F., & Graham, S. W. (1999). A model of college outcomes for adults. *Adult Education Quarterly, 50*(1), 24–40. https://doi.org/10.1177/074171369905000103

Heise, L. L. (1998). Violence against women: An integrated, ecological framework. *Violence against Women, 4*(3), 262–290. https://doi.org/10.1177/1077801298004003002

Lawton, M. P., & Nahemow, L. (1973). Ecology and the aging process. In C. Eisdorfer & M. P. Lawton (Eds.), *The psychology of adult development and aging* (pp. 619–674). American Psychological Association.

Moxley, D. P. (2000). Including homeless people with serious mental illness in the mental health system: A recovery-oriented approach. *Social Work, 45*(5), 522–531. https://doi.org/10.1093/sw/45.5.522

Phippen, A. (2016). *Children's online behaviour and safety: Policy and rights challenges*. Springer.

Phippen, A. (2025). *Policy and Rights Challenges in Children's Online Behaviour and Safety, 2017–2023*. Palgrave Macmillan.

Schaufeli, W. B., & Taris, T. W. (2014). A critical review of the Job Demands-Resources Model: Implications for improving work and health. In G. F. Bauer & O. Hämmig (Eds.), *Bridging occupational, organizational and public health* (pp. 43–68). Springer. https://doi.org/10.1007/978-94-007-5640-3_4

UK Government. (2015). *Criminal Justice and Courts Act 2015, c. 2, § 33*. https://www.legislation.gov.uk/ukpga/2015/2/section/33. Accessed May 2025.

UK Government. (2019). *Voyeurism (Offences) Act 2019*. https://www.legislation.gov.uk/ukpga/2019/2. Accessed May 2025.

UK Government. (2021). *Domestic Abuse Act 2021: Section 69*. Legislation.gov.uk. https://www.legislation.gov.uk/ukpga/2021/17/section/69/enacted. Accessed May 2025.

UK Government. (2023). *Online Safety Act 2023*. https://www.legislation.gov.uk/ukpga/2023/50. Accessed May 2025.

7

What Can Technology Actually Do to Tackle NCII?

Abstract This chapter critically examines the capabilities and limitations of technological interventions in addressing non-consensual intimate image (NCII) abuse. Focusing on tools such as perceptual hashing and the StopNCII.org platform, the chapter highlights how survivor-led, privacy-preserving technologies can support proactive content prevention when embedded in a broader ecosystem of support. It explores the evolution of platform liability and regulatory models like the UK's Online Safety Act and the EU Digital Services Act, arguing that while platform accountability is essential, it cannot replace systemic reforms in law enforcement, education, and victim services. Through an analysis of technological tools including AI and hash-matching, the chapter underscores that technological solutions alone cannot interpret the context and consent central to NCII. It introduces the concept of a self-certification scheme, proposing a legally backed mechanism that empowers individuals to declare specific content non-consensual and trigger automatic moderation. Ultimately, the chapter argues for a balanced, multi-stakeholder model where technology complements—but does not substitute for—legal, social, and cultural interventions.

S. Mortimer et al., *Ten Years of the Revenge Porn Helpline*, Palgrave Studies in Victims and Victimology, https://doi.org/10.1007/978-3-032-00614-1_7

Keywords Platform liability · Perceptual hashing · StopNCII.org · Survivor empowerment · Self-certification

As technology continues to evolve, so too do the forms of abuse it facilitates. While much attention has been paid to platform responsibility and regulatory intervention in recent years (Phippen, 2025), it is equally important to examine what technological tools themselves can realistically achieve in tackling harm. In the context of non-consensual intimate image (NCII) abuse, this means acknowledging both the promise and limitations of digital interventions.

This chapter explores the practical application of technology to NCII prevention, with a particular focus on the StopNCII initiative. Drawing on the experience of the UK Revenge Porn Helpline and its work with industry partners, the chapter examines how technical tools such as perceptual hashing have been used to support victims directly, without requiring them to surrender control over their images or engage repeatedly with platforms and law enforcement. StopNCII demonstrates how a victim-led, privacy—preserving tool can provide meaningful protection—if properly supported by a broader service ecosystem.

At the same time, the chapter considers what technology cannot do. Despite advances in artificial intelligence and automation, the nuances of consent, context, and harm remain challenging for machines to interpret. Calls for platform liability often overlook the complex social and legal realities of intimate image abuse, and there is a risk that over-reliance on technology diverts attention from other necessary supports: legal reform, education, victim services, and meaningful cultural change.

Throughout this discussion, the chapter also looks ahead asking whether the hashing-based model used by StopNCII could be expanded into a formal self-certification system. Such a system might allow victims to proactively register content as illegal, giving them greater agency and potentially overcoming the legal ambiguities that currently limit enforcement. While not without complications, it may offer a pragmatic route forward in a space where fully automated solutions remain legally and ethically constrained.

Ultimately, this chapter argues for a balanced view of technology—not as a silver bullet, but as one piece of a wider, multi-stakeholder response to technology-mediated abuse.

Platform Liability, Duty of Care, and the Policing of Online Harms

A key thread through this exploration of ten years of the Revenge Porn Helpline is how each victim has a different experience, and this is why a service like the Helpline is invaluable because practitioners can act as both a voice to victims and as a mediator to engage with other stakeholders. If a victim is turning to the Helpline as a last resort, or because they do not know what else to do, it is unquestionable that human support is most effective. However, that is not to say that some digital interventions are not useful tools to support the work of the helpline, and this final chapter explores technical inventions, and how they have evolved, at the Helpline over the last ten years, as well as consider what does, and does not work. In doing so, this chapter argues that an ecosystem where stakeholders can work in collaboration, bringing strength to solutions is a far more powerful model that the stakeholder scapegoating that besets the online harms world more generally.

As we discussed in Chapter 3 on policy and legal developments around IIA, in recent years, platform liability and duty of care have emerged as central legal frameworks in addressing online harms. These concepts place greater responsibility on digital platforms, requiring them to actively prevent, detect, and mitigate harmful content rather than merely acting as neutral intermediaries. Certainly, this shift marks a departure from early internet laws that provided platforms with broad immunity from liability for user-generated content and is arguably a reaction to this.

Historically, platforms operated under "safe harbour" provisions (Greer 2011). A safe harbour provision is a legal clause designed to protect individuals or organizations from liability when they meet specific conditions. It acts as a safeguard, allowing entities to operate without the constant threat of legal repercussions, if they adhere to certain rules. One of the most well-known examples of a safe harbour provision is found in the Digital Millennium Copyright Act (DMCA) (White, 2009), which shields online platforms like YouTube from direct liability for copyright infringement by their users. Under this provision, YouTube is not automatically responsible if a user upload copyrighted content without permission. However, to maintain this protection, the platform must follow strict guidelines. This includes implementing a system that allows copyright holders to submit takedown notices, promptly removing infringing content upon notification, and offering a dispute resolution process for users who believe their content was wrongly removed.

In considering safe harbour mechanisms around platform liability and harm to users, there have been traditional protections from liability with legislation such as Section 230 of the US Communications Decency Act (United States, 1996) and the EU E-Commerce Directive (European Union, 2000), both of which protected platforms from being held legally responsible for content posted by users (see Baistrocchi, 2002; Goldman, 2018). Under these early laws, platforms were only required to remove *illegal* material when notified. However, as digital spaces grew in influence, so did concerns about their role in facilitating harm and the problematic nature of safe harbour arrangements (Citron & Wittes, 2018). The argument that platforms were mere conduits for content became increasingly difficult to defend, particularly as issues such as terrorism, misinformation, child exploitation, and non-consensual intimate image abuse gained public and political attention.

This growing awareness has led to a shift towards greater platform accountability, with new laws requiring proactive content moderation, transparency in recommendation algorithms, and stricter enforcement against harmful material. The Online Safety Act 2023 (UK Government, 2023) is a key example of this approach, and it imposes a statutory duty of care on platforms, making them responsible for assessing and mitigating risks related to online harms. Similarly, the EU Digital Services Act (European Union, 2022) introduces a tiered system of obligations, with large platforms facing stricter requirements to prevent the spread of illegal and harmful content.

At the heart of this legal shift is the duty of care principle, which draws from traditional health and safety laws (Nolan, 2013). Just as employers have a duty to protect employees from foreseeable risks, digital platforms are now expected to anticipate, prevent, and mitigate potential harms to users. This does not mean they have to prevent all harm, but they must be able to demonstrate they have thought about the potential for harm and how they mitigate this. In this duty of care concept related to platform liability, there is debate over how to extend this beyond removing illegal content; within these emerging (and at the time of writing largely untested) approaches platforms must also conduct risk assessments, implement effective content moderation systems, and provide users with tools to report and filter harmful material so they are showing they are mindful to potential harms and understand their user base (Woods, 2019).

The rise of platform liability and duty of care as dominant regulatory approaches is driven by several factors. First, the sheer volume of online content makes traditional enforcement impractical, necessitating a model where platforms play a more active role in content governance. Second, the perceived failure of self-regulation (Cusumano et al., 2021) has fuelled public demand for stricter oversight (Trengove et al., 2022). While tech companies have long resisted regulation, high-profile incidents—such as the livestreamed Christchurch terrorist attack in 2019 and the spread of COVID-19 misinformation—have demonstrated, some argue (Marco-Franco et al., 2021; Thompson, 2019), the inadequacy of voluntary measures. Third, the disproportionate impact of online harms on women, minorities, and children has strengthened the case for stronger protections (Suzor et al., 2019).

The political and economic power of major technology companies has also contributed to this regulatory shift. Companies like Meta, Google, and TikTok have significant influence over public discourse, and policymakers argue that they have both the resources and the ethical responsibility to prevent harm (Rochefort, 2020). Additionally, the evolving understanding of online harms has broadened the scope of regulation. While early internet laws focused primarily on illegal content, modern legislation now addresses broader issues, including psychological distress, self-harm content, and algorithmic amplification of harmful material.

Regulatory competition among governments has further reinforced the dominance of platform liability and duty of care. The EU's Digital Services Act (European Union, 2022) and the UK's Online Safety Act (UK Government, 2023) set new standards for platform accountability, influencing other jurisdictions. And Australia's eSafety Commissioner has also introduced strong measures, including fines for platforms that fail to remove non-consensual intimate images (Smith et al., 2024). This international trend reflects a growing consensus that platform accountability is, politicians and regulators claim, essential for a safer online environment (Rochefort, 2020). However, the efficacy of these approaches remains to be seen, cases to date have in some cases been challenging (Phippen, 2024) and there have been predictions that this will simply move criticism from platforms to regulators (Phippen, 2025).

While these legal approaches might offer stronger protections, they also raise challenges and criticisms. One of the primary concerns is freedom of expression. Strict liability rules may lead to over-censorship, where platforms remove lawful but controversial content to avoid penalties (Judson et al., 2024). There are also concerns about the burden on smaller platforms, which may struggle to comply with complex regulations (Tyler et al., 2025). Additionally, the cross-border nature of digital platforms makes enforcement difficult, particularly when non-compliant services operate outside national jurisdictions. There have already been cases of regulatory overreach that demonstrate the potential for ethnocentric conflict (Phippen, 2024) where different regulators might demand conflicting responses to content they have, or haven't, deemed harmful.

The Limits of Platform Liability in Addressing Online Harms

The growing reliance on platform liability as a primary approach to online safety presents both an opportunity and a risk. While it is important digital platforms are accountable for the content they host, focusing too heavily on this aspect can distract from the broader systemic changes needed to effectively combat online harms.

The policy direction is, arguably, easier to mandate than to engage in the more challenging, long-term work of improving law enforcement responses, building more effective public education on these issues, and strengthening victim support services. This approach provides an immediate and tangible policy intervention and can be a more straightforward response to media and demands by charities to "do more" to prevent harms in a way that, for example, saying "we are building a more informed population to mitigate these risks" will not. However, there is a risk that such approaches will fail to address the root causes of harmful online behaviours and abuse, and we have discussed throughout this book that it is often stakeholders closer to the victim, such as law enforcement and peers, that fail in their duties as much as platforms.

Another factor driving this regulatory trend is the ease of enforcement. While governments can fine companies for failing to remove harmful content, it is much harder to change the attitudes of law enforcement officers who dismiss victims of online abuse, to provide adequate funding for frontline support organizations or to bring in the sort of progressive relationships education in schools that might go beyond victim-blaming and prohibitive narratives (Phippen, 2025). The reality is that even when harmful content is removed from a platform, the damage to the victim has often already been done and, as we have discussed, without proper legal, psychological, and financial support, their suffering continues and impact on victims can be severe. The issue does not go away simply because NCII has been removed by a platform, and if the justice system fails for example because of a police officer not taking a complaint seriously or a prosecutor deciding to not move to prosecute, the platform cannot be seen to be responsible for this. This is not to say that take down is not a crucial aspect of response and victim support. However, it is only one element.

The failure to improve law enforcement responses is one of the most glaring weaknesses of an over-reliance on platform liability. As we have discussed in previous chapters, many victims of non-consensual intimate image abuse, have reported that police officers do not take their cases seriously and even if the police make an arrest, this does not mean that prosecutors will agree with a move to prosecute. Freedom of Information data, we have presented shows that only a small fraction of complaints about intimate image abuse result in charges, despite the existence of laws criminalizing the behaviour. Instead of addressing these failures through specialized police training, better prosecutorial guidance, or dedicated cybercrime units, policymakers often focus on forcing platforms to act more quickly, which does little to help victims navigate the justice system or receive compensation.

Similarly, the underfunding of victim support services remains a critical problem. Funding challenges faced by the Helpline over the years are something we have discussed in previous chapters. Organizations that provide legal advice, psychological support, and practical assistance in removing harmful content have seen a surge in demand for their services, yet many continue to operate with budget levels set years ago. Instead of directing more resources to these essential services, governments tend to focus on platform liability as a frontline solution, shifting the burden onto private companies rather than ensuring victims receive the support they need.

Education is another area that is frequently overlooked in favour of punitive legal measures. While legislation can penalize those who engage in harmful online behaviour, prevention through education remains the most effective long-term strategy. Teaching young people about digital consent, online ethics, and the consequences of harmful behaviour could reduce the prevalence of online abuse at its source, yet this remains a low priority in many policy discussions as we have discussed in the previous chapter. Instead of investing in these preventative strategies, policymakers continue to focus on forcing platforms to remove harmful content after the damage has already been done.

Beyond legal and procedural gaps, cultural and societal attitudes towards online abuse remain a major barrier to meaningful change. Many forms of online harm, including deepfake pornography, cyberflashing, and image-based sexual abuse, are rooted in broader patterns of misogyny, exploitation, and power imbalances. Laws can criminalize individual acts, but they do not challenge the underlying societal norms that make these behaviours so prevalent.

While platform liability is a necessary part of the online safety landscape, it cannot be the sole solution. Governments that rely too heavily on regulating tech companies risk ignoring the structural failings that allow online harm to persist in the first place. If victim support remains underfunded, police fail to take cases seriously, and society does not address the root causes of abuse, no amount of platform regulation will meaningfully reduce harm. A truly effective response to online abuse requires a broader, multi-stakeholder approach-one that recognizes that laws alone cannot fix systemic failures, and that prevention, support, and education must be prioritized alongside enforcement.

Can NCII Be Made Illegal?

One scenario in tackling NCII which presents the limits of platform liability, at the present time, around take downs are the concerns and frustrations around non-compliant platforms hosting NCII. Often abroad, these sites will host NCII, and victims will inform the Helpline that their images are on these sites. However, as these platforms can rarely be legally reached, let alone be made to be compliant, they will often refuse take down requests. As we have discussed in previous chapters, there is a view that a model that works with Child Sexual Abuse Material (CSAM) should also be used for NCII. When policing CSAM content online, which is very clearly defined as illegal in UK, there are very clear expectations on service providers to remove content or, in the event that platforms are overseas, for UK based service providers to block access to these sites.

The Internet Watch Foundation (IWF)[1] operates as an independent body but collaborates closely with law enforcement agencies, internet service providers (ISPs), technology companies, and governments worldwide to achieve this.

One of its core functions is its URL blocking list.[2] This list contains web addresses that have been verified to host *illegal* content. The IWF constantly monitors the internet, identifying and verifying these URLs before adding them to the list. Only links that meet strict legal criteria are included, ensuring the system targets confirmed cases of CSAM.

Once compiled, the blocking list is distributed to internet service providers (ISPs), mobile network operators, and major technology companies that integrate it into their filtering systems. These organizations use the list to automatically block access to known CSAM websites. If a user attempts to visit a blocked URL, they may be redirected to a warning page explaining why access is restricted or be completely prevented from viewing the page, depending on how the ISP implements the block. This process significantly reduces the likelihood of people—whether intentionally or accidentally—coming into contact with CSAM.

In cases where an entire domain is found to be dedicated to distributing CSAM, the IWF and its partners take a broader approach by blocking the entire domain rather than just individual URLs. This is particularly important for hosted services-web hosts that repeatedly facilitate illegal content and refuse to cooperate with takedown requests. By blocking such domains at a network level, the IWF prevents offenders from simply moving content around within the same hosting environment, making it significantly harder for them to continue operating.

However, adopting a similar model for NCII presents some legal challenges that are not apparent for CSAM. CSAM as content is illegal and is relatively straightforward to define legally because it is the act taking place in the image that makes it illegal.

One of the greatest challenges in criminalizing Non-Consensual Intimate Images (NCII) is that the legality of the act is determined by

---

[1] https://www.iwf.org.uk/. Accessed May 2025.

[2] https://www.iwf.org.uk/our-technology/our-services/url-list/. Accessed May 2025.

consent rather than *content*. An identical image could be perfectly legal in one situation but illegal in another, depending entirely on whether the person depicted agreed to its distribution. This approach aims to protect personal privacy and prevent wrongful prosecution, but it also creates legal grey areas that make enforcement difficult. Since NCII laws do not, to date, criminalize the image itself, but rather its unauthorized sharing, platforms hosting such content may argue that the image itself is not illegal, making takedown requests more complicated.

This focus on consent rather than the nature of the image also places the burden of proof on victims, making it harder to seek justice, as we have explored in this book. Victims must often provide evidence that they did not consent, which can require exposing private conversations, prior agreements, or personal circumstances. If the NCII was originally shared in a private relationship, the perpetrator can claim they had permission at the time, making prosecution difficult. In some cases, the law requires proof that the image was shared with malicious intent, meaning perpetrators who distribute NCII without the explicit goal of harming the victim may not be held accountable. This loophole allows some offenders to escape legal consequences, even when their actions cause distress. Furthermore, many laws do not criminalize the threat of sharing NCII (sextortion), meaning offenders can use intimate images to coerce victims without technically breaking the law. Nevertheless, this legal hole has been addressed in current Scottish and English legislation.

The rise of AI-generated deepfake pornography has further exposed the weaknesses of consent-based NCII laws. Because deepfake NCII is created without an original image, many legal systems do not recognize it as a crime, even though it can cause just as much harm. Perpetrators often exploit this gap, claiming that their content is satire, free speech, or creative expression, making it harder to prosecute them (Meskys et al., 2020). However, focus on the content itself rather than consent, meaning any intimate image shared without explicit permission would be illegal, regardless of intent, would be practically extremely challenging. Such laws also raise concerns about over-policing, censorship, and potential criminalization of consensual sharing that later becomes contested. Without clearer legal definitions and stronger protections, many NCII cases will continue to fall through the cracks, leaving victims without justice.

Additionally, for CSAM website blocking decisions, these often happen without judicial oversight, leading to concerns that legitimate websites could be unfairly restricted (Nunziato, 2013). Unlike criminal investigations, where courts evaluate evidence, ISP blocking mechanisms are often based on lists compiled by governments or advocacy groups, which may lack transparency and accountability.

With NCII this becomes even more complex. For example, what if a website is unfairly accused of hosting NCII? Without clear appeals processes, lawful sites risk being blocked without justification. And what if an entire platform is blocked due to a small amount of NCII? Some user-generated content platforms (such as forums or image boards) may host both legal and illegal content, yet ISP-level blocking does not differentiate between them.

This creates a risk of over blocking, where access to innocent users, journalists, educators, and researchers is unfairly restricted, raising broader concerns about freedom of expression and censorship.

Fundamental to these debates is Net Neutrality (Cheng et al., 2011). This is a foundational principle of the online world that ISPs should treat all internet traffic equally, without discrimination, throttling, or blocking access to specific websites or services. The term was first coined by (Wu, 2003), where he argued that Internet service providers (ISPs) should treat all data on the Internet equally, without discriminating or charging differently based on user, content, website, or application. However, this principle does not extend protection to illegal content. Net neutrality was never intended to provide immunity for unlawful material such as child exploitation content or pirated media. ISPs are still required to comply with legal obligations, including court orders or government regulations that mandate the blocking or removal of such content.

At present, NCII (non-consensual intimate imagery) is not inherently illegal in the same way that CSAM (child sexual abuse material) is. This is because the content itself is not what makes it unlawful-rather, it is the act of sharing it without consent that constitutes the illegal behaviour. As a result, regulating NCII in the same manner as CSAM presents significant legal challenges. Asking ISPs to block websites hosting NCII directly challenges net neutrality, as it requires providers to actively intervene in how users access online content.

This is a central foundation on how the Internet operates. If ISPs are allowed to selectively block certain websites based upon demands extending beyond legal responsibilities, it sets a precedent for greater content control-potentially leading to political censorship, corporate favouritism, or suppression of dissenting voices. For example, who decides what gets blocked? If governments mandate website restrictions for NCII, which is not, of itself, illegal, and very difficult with current approaches to define illegal in terms of content, what prevents them from expanding such powers to other types of content (e.g. blocking news websites, political blogs, or opposition groups)? Many civil liberties organizations oppose ISP blocking because it undermines the open internet model, where users have the right to freely access and share information without interference (Thumfart, 2024).

This is not to say that because, currently, legal models for ISP level blocking would be extremely difficult for NCII, we should avoid it. Just that such approaches are not as simple as a rhetorical swipe in policy that simply states "we should make NCII illegal like CSAM and then ISPs must block it". We will explore potential approaches that might incorporate such approaches at the end of this chapter. For now, however, this discussion is put in place to illustrate the technical solutions to social problems are often far more complex that policy makers admit.

So What Can Platforms Actually Do?

What is typical when one raises opposition to an approach that extols platform liability is the pushback "so are you saying that platforms have no responsibility?" as if this is a binary choice—platforms should do nothing, or they should do everything. Of course this is not the case, and, as we will explore below, the helpline has both strong relationships with many platforms and makes significant use of technological tools to support victims. However, the Helpline, possibly because of being so close to victim support daily, understands the technology has strengths, and it has challenges, particularly in an area as complex and nuanced as IIA and NCII.

Platforms have a few things they can, and in some cases already do, in supporting victims of IIA. One of the most fundamental steps is the creation of strong and transparent policies that explicitly prohibit intimate image abuse. These policies should clearly define what constitutes a violation, reassuring victims that such content is not tolerated. Importantly, they must be easy to access and understand, ensuring that users can quickly find the necessary information when seeking help.

Platforms can also provide fast and accessible reporting mechanisms to enable victims to request the removal of harmful content as quickly as possible. While artificial intelligence approaches can play a key role in identifying and taking down abusive material before it spreads, this is not without its challenges, as we explore below. Hash-matching technology is another critical tool in preventing the spread of intimate image abuse and this is something we explore in far more detail below. Additionally, *trusted flagger programs* have been used by platforms for many years.

A Trusted Flagger Program is a system used by online platforms to more effectively identify and remove harmful or illegal content by prioritizing reports from selected users or organizations with a proven track record of accurate reporting. These trusted flaggers are often experts, nonprofits, government agencies, or highly active users who have demonstrated reliability in flagging content that violates platform policies. Because their reports are considered more credible, platforms typically review them more quickly and are more likely to act, such as removing posts, suspending accounts, or taking down videos. These programs are designed to help platforms manage the overwhelming volume of content shared every day, particularly when it involves sensitive issues like hate speech, terrorism-related material, child sexual abuse content, non-consensual intimate imagery, or misinformation (Appelman & Leerssen, 2022).

Several major online platforms have established trusted flagger programs that rely on partnerships with expert organizations to identify and report harmful or illegal content more effectively. On YouTube, the Trusted Flagger Program includes NGOs, government agencies, and academic institutions, with partners such as the Internet Watch Foundation (IWF) and INHOPE playing a key role in flagging material like child sexual abuse content.[3] At a broader regulatory level, the European Union's Digital Services Act (DSA) mandates that platforms engage with designated trusted flaggers-typically expert organizations with a proven ability to detect illegal content—ensuring their reports are prioritized and handled swiftly.

Of course, the Revenge Porn Helpline itself is an excellent example of a trusted flagger, and has worked for many years with a broad range of platforms to streamline the takedown process, ensuring swift action in urgent cases.

Beyond removal mechanisms, platforms must take steps to hold perpetrators accountable. This can involve IP tracking and account bans for repeat offenders, as well as coöperating with law enforcement when necessary. Strengthening penalties for policy violations, such as temporary or permanent suspensions, further deters abusive behaviour and signals a strong commitment to protecting users.

Finally, compliance with legal frameworks is essential. Platforms must adhere to national and international laws, such as the UK's Online Safety Act 2023 and the EU's Digital Services Act, ensuring that their policies align with evolving regulatory standards. Cooperation with law enforcement is particularly important in cases where legal action is necessary to hold perpetrators accountable.

The Challenges of Using AI

It is unquestionable that we are currently experiencing an AI renaissance, with rapid advancements in machine learning, generative AI, and automation reshaping industries, from healthcare and finance to creative arts and cybersecurity (Griffith & Metz, 2023).

However, AI is often proposed as a tool to moderate harmful content, detect Non-Consensual Intimate Images (NCII), or prevent the spread of misinformation, yet these systems still struggle with contextual nuance,

[3] https://transparency.google/intl/en-GB_ie/tools-programs/partner-programs/. Accessed May 2025.

false positives, and adversarial manipulation (Saeidnia et al., 2025). The over-reliance on AI without acknowledging its limitations risks creating flawed policies and assumed solutions that prioritize technological efficiency over human rights, fairness, and accountability.

An important aspect in understanding how AI might be used in tackling NCII requires us to understand how image recognition systems work, rather than the policy world simply saying, "use AI to recognize NCII". Artificial intelligence (AI)-driven image recognition systems will generally use machine learning (ML) and deep learning techniques to analyse visual data, identifying objects, patterns, and specific content in images or videos. These systems do not rely on manually programmed rules; instead, they learn by analysing large datasets (often referred to as *training data*), allowing them to detect specific features and classify images automatically.

The process begins with data collection and preprocessing. To train an AI model effectively, it requires a vast dataset of labelled images. For example, if an AI system is being developed to recognize cats, it must be exposed to thousands of labelled images of cats to learn what a "cat" looks like. Once the dataset is collected, the images undergo preprocessing, which involves standardizing their size, adjusting brightness and contrast to prevent biases, and performing data augmentation-introducing variations like rotation, flipping, and colour adjustments to improve the model's ability to recognize patterns under different conditions.

After preprocessing, the AI system begins feature extraction, where it identifies key visual patterns that distinguish objects. Rather than relying on predefined rules about what constitutes a cat, deep learning models (Li, 2022) automatically learn features from the dataset. These features start with simple elements like edges and shapes, then progress to more complex details such as textures, colours, and object structures. This hierarchical learning process enables the model to recognize objects at different levels of abstraction.

The next stage is model training, where systems process images through multiple layers. Convolutional layers (Liu, 2018) extract key features using filters that detect edges, textures, and patterns. Finally, fully connected layers make predictions based on all extracted features. The AI system continuously refines its accuracy through a process called backpropagation and optimization. Initially, the model makes predictions and compares them to the correct labels. Errors are calculated, and the model adjusts itself using gradient descent, repeating this process across millions of images until it reaches a high level of accuracy.

Once trained, the AI can be used for image classification and object detection. It can label an image ("cat" vs. "not cat"), detect specific objects within an image, or even segment an image, isolating a particular region (e.g. identifying a person's face separately from the background).

As we have stated, AI is very good at repetitive tasks with a recognizable behaviour set or image set. NCII has neither. What has become obvious over the years of the Helpline is there is no *typical* IIA case, all are different. Therefore, building training data so that a machine learning system can learn what features to recognize (either for image recognition or victim support) is very difficult. Consider also how an image recognition system might build a training dataset—would it be possible for a platform or vendor to be able to collect a large training data set of NCII without considerable ethical and legal challenges around consent to use images and the privacy rights of the victims?

One of AI's fundamental weaknesses is its inability to interpret *context* when identifying intimate images. One form of context might be that of consent. While machine learning models can recognize nudity and explicit content, they cannot determine consent. AI lacks the ability to differentiate between a private intimate image willingly shared between partners and one that has been leaked without consent. In both cases, the image itself may appear identical, yet only one constitutes abuse.

This limitation could extend to misinterpretation of legitimate content. If an AI systems would mistakenly flag artistic photography, medical images, or sexual health education materials as NCII, this might lead to wrongful content removal. Additionally, AI struggles to assess *intent*—whether an image was uploaded maliciously to harm someone or was posted by the individual themselves. Unlike human moderators who can analyse captions, comments, and user behaviour, AI lacks the ability to distinguish consensual sharing from harmful misuse, leading to both false positives (incorrectly flagged content) and false negatives (missed NCII cases). Moreover, NCII comes in many forms, often involving partially clothed images or culturally sensitive content, which AI may overlook if trained solely on explicit nudity. Building effective training datasets is also ethically and legally challenging, given the privacy rights of victims and the difficulty in obtaining consent.

An Alternative Approach

StopNCII.org has been mentioned at various points through this book and is now a system fundamental to victim support and the services offered by the Helpline. It is an international platform aimed at reducing the spread of non-consensual intimate images (NCII) by providing a technical mechanism for individuals to prevent the online distribution of their private images. Operated by the Revenge Porn Helpline the platform, developed with a significant in kind contribution from Meta, allows users to create cryptographic hashes (Farid, 2021)—digital fingerprints—of images on their own devices. These hashes, not the images themselves, are shared with participating technology companies, enabling them to detect and block matching content across their platforms.

StopNCII uses perceptual hashing, which analyses the visual features of an image rather than its exact data. This allows for the detection of modified versions of the same image, such as those that have been cropped or altered in brightness or colour. Participating platforms uploaded content against the hash database and can prevent the distribution of content that matches a known hash.

Importantly, the original images are never uploaded or stored, addressing privacy concerns. The irreversible nature of the hashing process ensures that the original image cannot be reconstructed from the hash. While this approach does not prevent all instances of NCII—particularly those involving entirely new or unseen content—it provides a means for users to take pre-emptive steps to reduce the likelihood of their images being shared without consent.

We have already discussed hashing above, in the context of the IWF, in preventing the dissemination of CSAM. It is a tried and tested approach to identifying illegal content and is effective on an international platform. Put simply, hashing is a process in cryptography that transforms input data (such as an image, file, or text) into a fixed-length string of characters, called a hash value. This hash acts as a digital fingerprint, uniquely representing the original data. One of the key properties of hashing is that it is one-way and irreversible—meaning that once data is hashed, it cannot be reconstructed back into the original file. Traditional cryptographic hashing algorithms, such as MD5 or SHA-256, generate unique hashes for specific files. Therefore, the slightest change to the file—such as modifying a single pixel or adjusting brightness—produces an entirely different hash. While this method is effective for verifying exact matches, it is not useful when dealing with altered or modified images, which is a common tactic used by perpetrators of intimate image abuse.

To address this limitation, the IWF and StopNCII.org use a specialized form of hashing known as perceptual hashing (iBid.). Unlike traditional hashing, perceptual hashing analyses the actual content and visual structure of an image rather than just the raw data. This allows it to generate hashes that are resistant to minor modifications. For example, if an intimate image is slightly cropped, resized, or adjusted in colour, the perceptual hash will still recognize it as being derived from the original, allowing platforms to detect and block altered versions of the same image.

Given the more legally complex nature of NCII, compared to CSAM, the approach to hashing for StopNCII.org differs. Rather than having analysts identify and hash illegal content, StopNCII.org empowers victims by providing them with the means to hash their own images without having to share them with a third party. When an individual wants to prevent their intimate images from being shared, they use StopNCII.org's tool to create a hash of the image directly on their own device. This means that the original image never leaves their phone or computer-only the hash is generated and stored. Once the hash is created, it is securely submitted to StopNCII.org's database. Participating platforms, such as Facebook, Instagram, TikTok, Pornhub, and Reddit, have access to this database and continuously check uploaded content against these stored hashes. If an attempt is made to upload an image that matches a stored hash, the platform can automatically block or remove the content before it is shared. And because hashing is irreversible, there is no way for anyone—including StopNCII.org or tech platforms—to recover the original image from the hash. This means that even if the hash database were compromised, the original images would remain completely private.

The key benefit of using perceptual hashing in the fight against intimate image abuse is that it allows for proactive prevention. Rather than requiring victims to report violations after their images have already been circulated, StopNCII.org enables them to pre-emptively block their images from being shared in the first place.

Additionally, the collaborative effort between StopNCII.org and major tech companies ensures that once an image is hashed and submitted, it is monitored across multiple platforms, reducing the chances of it being spread across the internet. By leveraging the making use of established technology that has been proven to work in other use cases, StopNCII.org provides a secure, private, and effective way for victims to reclaim control over their personal content.

As of November 2024, StopNCII.org has facilitated the creation of over 1,000,000 unique hashes to protect individuals from non-consensual intimate image (NCII) abuse.[4]

While adopting a hashing approach to protecting victims of NCII is, arguably, more effective than relying on less predictable technology such as AI, it is not without technical and cultural risks. While StopNCII.org is designed with privacy and victim safety at its core—ensuring that original images never leave a user's device and only hashes are shared—it still operates within the broader ecosystem of hash-based detection systems and is therefore subject to many of the same concerns.

For instance, database integrity remains a key issue. Although StopNCII.org uses perceptual hashing to account for minor image alterations, its effectiveness still depends on the accuracy and security of its hash database. If this database were compromised—through unauthorized modification of hashes—it could result in either the wrongful blocking of innocent content or the failure to stop the distribution of actual NCII material.

[4] https://saferinternet.org.uk/blog/stopncii-org-marks-major-milestone-in-the-fight-against-non-consensual-intimate-image-abuse. Accessed May 2025.

There are also broader privacy and surveillance concerns, particularly regarding scope creep. StopNCII.org is explicitly focused on protecting victims of NCII, but as perceptual hashing technology becomes more widely adopted across different sectors, there is a legitimate concern that such tools could be repurposed beyond their original intent (Martin, 2018). If safeguards are not maintained, the same infrastructure could hypothetically be used to flag or monitor other types of content, including political or personal material, raising questions about oversight and accountability.

Finally, legal and ethical issues around hash-based takedown systems also apply. Although StopNCII.org is privacy-preserving by design, the absence of transparency into how platforms respond to hash matches, or what redress mechanisms exist if content is wrongfully blocked, could present challenges especially in contexts where definitions of "intimate" or "non-consensual" may vary culturally or legally.

Concerns About Hash Inversion

Perceptual hashing has become a core element of image-based abuse prevention, including tools like StopNCII.org. These hashes, derived through algorithms such as Microsoft's PhotoDNA or Facebook's PDQ, are designed to be non-invertible-that is, they cannot be reversed to reconstruct the original image. Traditionally, it has been assumed that perceptual hashes cannot be used to recreate the original image because they reduce a rich image file—often hundreds of kilobytes or megabytes—to just a few dozen bytes. This reduction discards most pixel-level data, leaving only abstract representations of visual features such as contrast, edges, or luminance patterns. As such, inversion has long been considered computationally and mathematically infeasible.

However, recent developments in machine learning, particularly the use of Generative Adversarial Networks (GANs) has raised questions about whether this claim holds universally—especially in the sensitive context of Non-Consensual Intimate Images (NCII). A recent study (Hawkes et al., 2024) demonstrated that it is possible to approximate original images from perceptual hash values using machine learning. The researchers trained a Pix2Pix-based GAN on a large public dataset of celebrity faces (CelebA) to infer visual features from known hash values. They were able to reconstruct images that, while not identical, retained significant identifiable features such as facial structure, skin tone, and clothing. In some cases, reconstructed images reached high levels of perceptual similarity with the originals. The suggestion in the paper was that, given the success in reconstructing faces, there is a potential risk in the use of perceptual hashing in NCII.

However, while the inversion of perceptual hashes is demonstrably possible in controlled research environments, applying these methods to NCII is far more complex, for several reasons:

- Lack of Public Datasets: The study mentioned above relied on large, publicly available datasets (e.g. CelebA), which contain high-quality, consistently formatted images. No such datasets exist for NCII-nor should they, due to the ethical and legal implications. Without large, labelled training data of NCII, training an inversion model becomes far more difficult.
- Variability of NCII Content: NCII spans a wide range of images, from selfies in private spaces to webcam captures or cropped screenshots. These vary dramatically in quality, framing, lighting, and context. Unlike the relatively uniform training data used in facial recognition studies, NCII content lacks visual consistency, making it harder for machine learning models to learn patterns that could support reliable inversion.
- Consent and Context Are Irreproducible: Even if an image's broad features were reconstructed, critical contextual information—such as consent, intent, and personal history—cannot be inferred from a hash. This undermines the idea that any reverse-engineered image could meaningfully "recreate" NCII content in a way that would be legally or ethically actionable.
- Perceptual Hash Function Choice Matters: The success of inversion also depends heavily on which hashing algorithm is used. The study showed that some functions (like aHash or NeuralHash) were more vulnerable to inversion than others. PhotoDNA produced less detailed

reconstructions, though not immune. The level of resistance varies—indicating that some systems are more robust than others, but none are entirely secure.

From a theoretical perspective, the article has shown hash inversion is possible. Machine learning techniques can generate images that match the perceptual hash of a known image, particularly when trained on similar datasets. Reconstruction of faces, particularly those that can be drawn from a public database does not mean that NCII would be as possible. However, in the specific context of NCII, the practical risk is currently low, due to the absence of accessible training data at sufficient volume, legal barriers to data collection, and the immense variability in NCII content.

That said, the privacy implications are serious. Even the possibility that perceptual hashes could reveal identifying features of intimate content means that hashes should be treated as sensitive data.

Self-Certification—A Possible Next Step?

StopNCII.org has demonstrated the power of stakeholders in the ecosystem working to their strengths for a common goal. We have, in this chapter, also highlighted the challenges in handing the control of content that is not, of itself, illegal but becomes illegal if non-consensually shared, back to the subject of these images. A self-certification scheme for non-consensual intimate image (NCII) abuse offers a transformative step towards a more survivor-led, proactive, and systematized approach to protecting individuals from image-based harm. Unlike current frameworks—which are heavily reliant on victims navigating fragmented platform policies or criminal justice systems—self-certification would allow individuals to formally declare certain images as non-consensual, thereby triggering automatic or rapid protective measures across digital platforms.

At the heart of the scheme is the principle of survivor empowerment. Individuals who fear their intimate images may be shared without consent—or who know that such a breach has occurred—would be able to take action themselves without needing to upload sensitive content or prove criminal intent. Instead, the process would begin on the victim's own device, using secure technology to create a unique digital fingerprint or "hash" of the image. The image itself would never leave the device, preserving privacy and security. The individual would then complete a formal declaration-a digital affidavit-affirming that they appear in the image, that it is intimate in nature, and that it was or could be shared without their consent.

This declaration and corresponding hash would be submitted to a secure, centralized database operated by a trusted intermediary-potentially an expanded version of StopNCII.org or a newly created international clearinghouse. Importantly, the database would serve not just as a repository for matching purposes, but as a recognized legal register. With the appropriate legislation in place, the act of self-certifying an image in this way would give it a recognized legal status as unlawful to distribute, compelling platforms to act swiftly and consistently.

Participating platforms would integrate this system into their moderation pipelines. Again, this is a model that has already been demonstrated to be successful with StopNCII.org. Every time a new piece of content is uploaded, it would be automatically scanned against the hash database. If a match is found, the image could be immediately blocked, flagged for review, or subject to automatic takedown. This process would apply across participating services, creating consistency where there is currently fragmentation and vastly reducing the burden on victims to make individual complaints to multiple platforms.

The model would also allow for a pre-emptive approach. Victims anticipating a potential leak—such as in cases of abusive relationships, blackmail, or threats to share—could register images before they are ever uploaded online. If someone later attempted to post the content, the platform would detect the match and prevent publication. In this way, self-certification not only addresses current harm but can also play a critical role in prevention.

Of course, such a scheme must include robust safeguards to prevent misuse. It is vital that only those who appear in the image can certify it as non-consensual. Verification steps—such as secure identity checks, biometric matching, or third-party helpline mediation—would need to be built in to ensure authenticity without introducing barriers for victims. Oversight by a neutral, survivor-trusted body would be essential, and victims must have access to appeals processes and clear pathways to support if platforms fail to respond appropriately.

Importantly, self-certification must be backed by legislation that formalizes its authority and mandates platform participation. This legal recognition would transform the system from a helpful but voluntary tool into an enforceable right. It would also allow regulatory bodies, such as Ofcom in the UK or equivalent agencies globally, to monitor compliance and impose sanctions where necessary.

In sum, a self-certification scheme would fundamentally reframe the dynamics of NCII response. Rather than requiring victims to rely on slow, often retraumatizing takedown processes or criminal investigations with low success rates, this model gives them a direct, protective mechanism rooted in dignity and control. It complements existing legal frameworks but fills a critical gap: enabling rapid, scalable action while respecting privacy and autonomy. With proper governance, technological infrastructure, and legal backing, self-certification offers a practical, survivor-centred solution to one of the most pervasive digital harms of our time.

Conclusions

Technology has a crucial, yet inherently limited, role in supporting victims of non-consensual intimate image (NCII) abuse—as we have shown in the ecosystem model in Chapter 6—this is not an issue that can be resolved by one stakeholder. As this chapter has explored, tools like StopNCII.org demonstrate the real and immediate benefits of victim-led, privacy-preserving technological interventions. Perceptual hashing, in particular, allows for the proactive prevention of harm across multiple platforms without requiring survivors to relinquish control over their images. These innovations show that, when thoughtfully designed and ethically implemented, technology can help return agency to victims and reduce the circulation of abusive content at scale.

However, technology is not a panacea. Automated systems—even the most sophisticated AI—struggle with the contextual complexities that define NCII. The very nature of intimate image abuse, rooted in consent, power dynamics, and evolving forms of exploitation, resists purely computational solutions. Over-reliance on AI or platform moderation risks sidelining the critical social, legal, and cultural reforms needed to support victims fully. As seen throughout this chapter, the most effective interventions emerge when technology operates within a broader ecosystem of support-one that includes education, law enforcement reform, victim services, and meaningful regulatory oversight.

A future-facing approach, such as the proposed self-certification model, offers a compelling path forward. It suggests how technical tools can go beyond harm response to empower individuals and assert legal agency over their digital selves. Yet, such models require significant legal, infrastructural, and ethical scaffolding. Without legislative backing, platform cooperation, and strong data protections, even the most well-intentioned technological solutions may falter.

Ultimately, the lesson is clear: technology can help—sometimes profoundly—but it cannot substitute for systemic change. Tools like StopNCII.org must be seen not as endpoints, but as part of a collaborative, survivor-centred response to online abuse. If we treat technology as a partner in justice rather than a solution in itself, it can support—not supplant—the deeper cultural and institutional shifts that are truly needed.

References

Appelman, N., & Leerssen, P. (2022). On "Trusted" Flaggers. *Yale Journal of Law & Technology, 24*, 452.

Baistrocchi, P. A. (2002). Liability of intermediary service providers in the EU Directive on Electronic Commerce. *Santa Clara Computer and High Technology Law Journal, 19*, 111.

Cheng, H. K., Bandyopadhyay, S., & Guo, H. (2011). The debate on net neutrality: A policy perspective. *Information Systems Research, 22*(1), 60–82.

Citron, D. K., & Wittes, B. (2018). The problem isn't just backpage: Revising Section 230 immunity. *Georgetown Law Technology Review, 2*(2), 453.
Cusumano, M. A., Gawer, A., & Yoffie, D. B. (2021). Can self-regulation save digital platforms? *Industrial and Corporate Change, 30*(5), 1259–1285.
European Union. (2000). *Directive 2000/31/EC of the European Parliament and of the Council of 8 June 2000 on certain legal aspects of information society services, in particular electronic commerce, in the Internal Market (Directive on electronic commerce).* https://eur-lex.europa.eu/eli/dir/2000/31/oj
European Union. (2022). *Regulation (EU) 2022/2065 of the European Parliament and of the Council of 19 October 2022 on a Single Market for Digital Services and amending Directive 2000/31/EC (Digital Services Act).* https://eur-lex.europa.eu/eli/reg/2022/2065/oj
Farid, H. (2021). An overview of perceptual hashing. *Journal of Online Trust and Safety, 1*(1).
Goldman, E. (2018). The complicated story of FOSTA and section 230. *First Amendment Law Review, 17*, 279.
Greer, D. (2011). Safe Harbor—A framework that works. *International Data Privacy Law, 1*(3), 143–148.
Griffith, E., & Metz, C. (2023, January). A new area of AI booms, even amid the tech gloom. *New York Times*, 7.
Hawkes, S., Weinert, C., Almeida, T., & Mehrnezhad, M. (2024). Perceptual hash inversion attacks on image-based sexual abuse removal tools. *IEEE Security & Privacy.*
Judson, E., Kira, B., & Howard, J. W. (2024). The bypass strategy: Platforms, the online safety act and future of online speech. *Journal of Media Law*, 1–22.
Liu, Y. H. (2018). Feature extraction and image recognition with convolutional neural networks. In *Journal of Physics: Conference Series* (Vol. 1087, p. 062032). IOP Publishing.
Li, Y. (2022). Research and application of deep learning in image recognition. In *2022 IEEE 2nd international conference on power, electronics and computer applications (ICPECA)* (pp. 994–999). IEEE.
Marco-Franco, J. E., Pita-Barros, P., Vivas-Orts, D., González-de-Julián, S., & Vivas-Consuelo, D. (2021). COVID-19, fake news, and vaccines: Should regulation be implemented? *International Journal of Environmental Research and Public Health, 18*(2), 744.
Martin, D. (2018). Demystifying Hash Searches. *Stanford Law Review, 70*, 691.

Meskys, E., Kalpokiene, J., Jurcys, P., & Liaudanskas, A. (2020). Regulating deep fakes: Legal and ethical considerations. *Journal of Intellectual Property Law & Practice, 15*(1), 24–31.

Nolan, D. (2013). Deconstructing the duty of care. *Law Quarterly Review, 129*, 559–575.

Nunziato, D. C. (2013). The beginning of the end of internet freedom. *Georgetown Journal of International Law, 45*, 383.

Phippen, A. (2024). The broken online safety ecosystem. *Entertainment Law Review, 35*(7).

Phippen, A. (2025). *Policy and rights challenges in children's online behaviour and safety, 2017–2023.* Springer Nature Switzerland.

Rochefort, A. (2020). Regulating social media platforms: A comparative policy analysis. *Communication Law and Policy, 25*(2), 225–260.

Saeidnia, H. R., Hosseini, E., Lund, B., Tehrani, M. A., Zaker, S., & Molaei, S. (2025). Artificial intelligence in the battle against disinformation and misinformation: a systematic review of challenges and approaches. *Knowledge and Information Systems*, 1–20.

Smith, M., Nolan, M., & Gaffey, J. (2024). Online safety and social media regulation in Australia: eSafety Commissioner v X Corp. *Griffith Law Review, 33*(1), 2–18.

Suzor, N., Dragiewicz, M., Harris, B., Gillett, R., Burgess, J., & Van Geelen, T. (2019). Human rights by design: The responsibilities of social media platforms to address gender-based violence online. *Policy & Internet, 11*(1), 84–103.

Thompson, P. A. (2019). Beware of geeks bearing gifts: Assessing the regulatory response to the Christchurch Call. *The Political Economy of Communication, 7*(1).

Thumfart, J. (2024). Net neutrality, state neutrality, and neutralization. In *The Liberal internet in the postliberal era: Digital sovereignty, private government, and practices of neutralization* (pp. 141–184). Springer Nature Switzerland.

Trengove, M., Kazim, E., Almeida, D., Hilliard, A., Zannone, S., & Lomas, E. (2022). A critical review of the Online Safety Bill. *Patterns, 3*(8).

Tyler, T., Meares, T., & Katsaros, M. (2025). New worlds arise: Online trust and safety. *Annual Review of Criminology, 8*.

UK Government. (2015). *Criminal Justice and Courts Act 2015, c. 2, § 33.* https://www.legislation.gov.uk/ukpga/2015/2/section/33. Accessed May 2025.

UK Government. (2019). *Voyeurism (Offences) Act 2019.* https://www.legislation.gov.uk/ukpga/2019/2. Accessed May 2025.

UK Government. (2021). *Domestic Abuse Act 2021: Section 69*. Legislation.gov.uk. https://www.legislation.gov.uk/ukpga/2021/17/section/69/enacted. Accessed May 2025.

UK Government. (2023). *Online Safety Act 2023*. https://www.legislation.gov.uk/ukpga/2023/50. Accessed May 2025.

United States. (1996). *47 U.S.C. § 230 – Protection for private blocking and screening of offensive material*. https://www.law.cornell.edu/uscode/text/47/230

White, B. (2009). Viacom v. YouTube: A proving ground for DMCA safe harbors against secondary liability. *St. John's Journal of Legal Commentary, 24*, 811.

Woods, L. (2019). *Online harm reduction—A statutory duty of care and regulator*. Available at SSRN 4003986.

Wu, T. (2003). Network neutrality, broadband discrimination. *Journal on Telecommunications & High Technology Law, 2*, 141.

8

Conclusions and the Future

Abstract This chapter concludes the book by synthesizing a decade of research, frontline practice, and policy engagement through the lens of the UK's Revenge Porn Helpline (RPH), positioning intimate image abuse (IIA) as a pervasive, gendered, and systemic digital harm. It reflects on the evolution of IIA from a misunderstood phenomenon to a global human rights concern, highlighting the RPH's pivotal role in driving legal reform, victim support, and technological innovation. The chapter outlines key findings from previous chapters, emphasizing the need for multilayered responses across legal, cultural, institutional, and technological systems. It proposes ambitious international recommendations, including a Five Eyes NCII Clearing Centre, mandated platform integration with StopNCII.org, legal harmonization through cybercrime treaties, and the development of a victim-led self-certification system. Ultimately, the chapter argues that a coordinated, survivor-centred, and globally integrated approach is essential to achieving justice, prevention, and dignity in the digital age.

Keywords Global governance · Survivor-centred response · StopNCII.org · Legal harmonization · Intimate image abuse policy reform

S. Mortimer et al., *Ten Years of the Revenge Porn Helpline*, Palgrave Studies in Victims and Victimology, https://doi.org/10.1007/978-3-032-00614-1_8

This book has traced the emergence, expansion, and institutionalization of the UK's Revenge Porn Helpline (RPH) over the past decade, drawing together legal analysis, frontline service data, and international comparisons to present a comprehensive account of intimate image abuse (IIA) as one of the defining digital harms of our time. As the preceding chapters have demonstrated, IIA has evolved from a poorly understood and narrowly defined criminal phenomenon—mischaracterised under the banner of "revenge porn"—into a multifaceted and globally distributed pattern of abuse. The Helpline's trajectory exemplifies how an initially modest intervention, rooted in practical victim support, can transform into a pivotal actor in shaping policy, law, and technological responses.

Chapter 2 provided a foundational narrative of the RPH's operational journey. Initially launched as a one-year pilot, it responded to a glaring service gap for adult victims of IIA—particularly women who faced online abuse with little recourse. What began as a reactive service for takedown assistance evolved into a strategic institution embedded in the online safety infrastructure. Through close partnerships with government, law enforcement, civil society, and major tech platforms, the Helpline has become a global reference point for victim support models and proactive harm prevention. The COVID-19 pandemic marked a key inflection point, accelerating digital harms and increasing demand for services, while reinforcing the limitations of existing legal and institutional protections.

Chapter 3 offered a critical legal history of IIA in the UK, demonstrating that legislative responses have been largely reactive, often constrained by narrow definitions and rooted in outdated assumptions about victim culpability and offender intent. While the Criminal Justice and Courts Act 2015 was a landmark in recognizing the harm of non-consensual image sharing, its requirement for "intent to cause distress" and its exclusion of threats and synthetic media soon revealed its shortcomings. The chapter detailed how RPH casework provided the evidentiary base for later reforms, including the Domestic Abuse Act 2021 and Online Safety Act 2023, both of which expanded legal recognition of the scope and mechanisms of abuse.

Chapter 4 shifted focus to the lived experiences of victims, drawing from qualitative case narratives, court data, and testimonies to highlight the gaps between legal reform and justice in practice. Despite legislative advances, many victims continue to encounter barriers in the form of police inaction, re-traumatization through criminal processes, and minimal sentencing outcomes. The chapter called for a trauma-informed and survivor-centred justice model—one that acknowledges the cumulative and ongoing nature of digital harm, and places recovery and agency at its centre, not solely retribution.

In Chapter 5, the book interrogated the socio-cultural dimensions of IIA, drawing on intersectional analysis to show how gender, race, class, sexuality, and disability influence the forms and consequences of abuse. It challenged the archetype of the "ideal victim" and demonstrated how underrepresented groups—including LGBTQ+ individuals, women of colour, and disabled women-face compounded barriers to support, recognition, and redress. The chapter emphasized the importance of culturally competent services, representative data collection, and targeted outreach in both service delivery and research.

Chapter 6 advanced a theoretical shift by situating IIA within Bronfenbrenner's ecological systems framework. Rather than treating digital abuse as isolated incidents, this model highlights the interconnected layers of influence: individual behaviour, interpersonal dynamics, institutional responses, cultural norms, and digital infrastructures. The chapter argued that systemic solutions must engage across all these layers simultaneously, rather than relying exclusively on criminalization or individualistic narratives of blame and shame.

In Chapter 7, the book turned to the technological frontier, evaluating how tools like perceptual hashing, digital fingerprinting, and AI-assisted moderation have altered the terrain of image-based abuse prevention. It detailed the development of *StopNCII.org* as a transformative initiative: a decentralized, privacy-preserving platform designed to allow users to prevent the upload of intimate images across multiple platforms without ever sharing those images. Yet the chapter also sounded notes of caution, stressing that technical solutions must be embedded within broader regulatory, ethical, and human-centred frameworks to avoid reproducing harm or excluding marginalized users.

Across these chapters, several common threads emerge:

1. **IIA is a gendered, systemic, and globally pervasive harm.** While it manifests differently across regions and populations, it is overwhelmingly targeted at women and structurally facilitated by platform architectures, cultural stigma, and legislative inertia.
2. **Victim support cannot be disentangled from law, technology, or culture.** The RPH demonstrates the need for integrated, interdisciplinary, and survivor-centred responses that combine frontline care with upstream prevention and systems-level change.
3. **Data, if ethically collected and interpreted, is a source of power.** The Helpline's role as both a support service and knowledge producer has been essential in shifting legal definitions, platform policies, and public understanding of digital abuse.
4. **Prevention is possible, but only through coordinated international effort.** Tools like StopNCII.org show that proactive systems can stop harm before it begins but only if they are widely adopted, and preferably enforced through legislation.

This book has served not only as a retrospective on ten years of pioneering work, but also as a roadmap for the next ten. The challenges ahead are significant: closing global reporting gaps, standardising enforcement, embedding digital literacy into education, and dismantling the social norms that sustain image-based abuse. Yet, the progress achieved thus far—against a backdrop of institutional resistance, rapid technological change, and underfunding—is a testament to what is possible when victim-survivors, researchers, practitioners, and policy actors work in concert.

Ultimately, this is not just a story of digital harm. It is a story of digital citizenship, gender justice, and the right to privacy and dignity in an increasingly surveilled and information dense world. The future of online safety will depend not only on innovation or regulation, but on a collective reimagining across the ecosystem of what it means to be safe and respected in a connected culture.

At the start of this book, we aimed to attempt to quantify the scale of the NCII problem. The modelling applied in the opening analysis highlights the vast scale of the issue, demonstrating that NCII is at least as prevalent as CSAM and yet lacks the same level of international coordination, legislative mandates, and enforcement mechanisms. Our findings confirm that NCII remains significantly underreported, with tens of millions of victims likely affected worldwide every year.

Throughout this book, we have expanded upon the data presented, incorporating extensive quantitative and qualitative evidence to highlight the profound individual impact of NCII, the legal ambiguities and shortcomings that persist, and the urgent need for a comprehensive, multi-stakeholder response. The evidence clearly reinforces the necessity for a coordinated international approach to address the escalating NCII crisis.

With nearly a decade of legislative experience in tackling NCII, the UK, and more specifically the Helpline, is uniquely positioned to lead efforts in shaping a global response. The recommendations outlined here demonstrate the critical need for scalable intervention strategies. Specifically, we propose the following:

1. Establishing a Five Eyes NCII Clearing Centre: The creation of a centralized Non-Consensual Intimate Image (NCII) Clearing Centre among Five Eyes member states could serve as a pilot initiative to enhance cross-border coordination and develop scalable governance frameworks. Modelled on the success of the US National Centre for Missing and Exploited Children (NCMEC)—which has effectively centralized and mandated reporting of child sexual abuse material (CSAM)—this approach holds the potential to significantly strengthen international NCII response mechanisms. Considering the existing collaboration between StopNCII.org and NCMEC's *Take It Down* platform, this clearing centre could standardize reporting procedures, enhance cooperation among law enforcement agencies, and broaden the provision of victim support services across participating jurisdictions.
2. Scaling StopNCII.org as a Global Reporting Infrastructure: StopNCII.org has emerged as a leading global resource for NCII victim support, leveraging innovative device-side hashing technology to prevent the re-distribution of intimate images. To fully realize its

potential, legal mandates should require digital platforms to integrate with this system, thereby facilitating the proactive identification, removal, and reporting of NCII content. Establishing global obligations for platform integration would promote a standardized, effective, and victim-centred approach to content moderation, reducing the burden on affected individuals while raising industry-wide accountability.

3. Enhancing Victim Support Services: With projected increases in NCII cases, existing victim support services—such as the Revenge Porn Helpline—will require substantial investment to expand their operational capacity and technological infrastructure. Priorities should include the development of automated reporting mechanisms, advanced content detection tools, and platform-level response systems to ensure the prompt and effective removal of harmful content. Strengthening these resources is essential to delivering timely assistance and safeguarding the well-being of NCII victims.
4. Embedding NCII Enforcement in International Cybercrime Frameworks: Integrating NCII-specific provisions into international cybercrime treaties, in collaboration with United Nations agencies and transnational law enforcement bodies, is critical to achieving a coordinated global response. This should involve the implementation of mandatory reporting obligations, harmonized standards for victim assistance, and capacity-building efforts in under-resourced jurisdictions. Key strategies include targeted training programs, investment in investigative technologies, and the establishment of robust channels for international cooperation—ensuring a consistent and sustainable global framework for addressing NCII.

Furthermore, we would make the following broader policy recommendations as a result of the research presented in this book:

Mandate Platform Integration with StopNCII.org
The book highlights the success of StopNCII.org, a privacy-preserving tool that prevents the re-upload of harmful content. To scale this globally, the authors recommend legal mandates requiring all major platforms to integrate with it. This would shift responsibility to

tech companies, enabling faster, victim-driven content takedown and ensuring consistent protection regardless of the platform used.

Embed NCII Protections in International Cybercrime Frameworks
A strong recommendation is to integrate NCII offences into global cybercrime treaties, such as the forthcoming UN Cybercrime Convention. Doing so would harmonize legal definitions, require mandatory reporting, and ensure minimum standards for victim support worldwide. This measure is essential for jurisdictions where current legal protections are absent or fragmented.

Substantially Increase Funding for Victim Support Services
With NCII cases rapidly rising, services like the UK's Revenge Porn Helpline are under immense pressure. The book calls for stable, multi-year funding to expand these services, invest in better technology, and hire more trained staff. Without adequate funding, legal and technical reforms cannot reach their full potential to support survivors.

Standardize and Expand Legal Definitions
The authors call for comprehensive legislative reform to include threats to share, deepfakes, and altered images under NCII laws. This also includes removing requirements such as proving "intent to cause distress", which previously hindered prosecutions. Consistency across jurisdictions is critical, both within the UK and internationally.

Introduce a Self-Certification System for Victim-Led Content Takedown
A novel proposal is the development of a self-certification model that enables victims to assert control over their digital selves. This approach bypasses the often retraumatizing legal process by giving survivors a fast, secure way to block content before it's uploaded-reframing prevention as a right rather than a reactive service.

Reform Law Enforcement and Judicial Practices
The book underscores the systemic failure of police and prosecutors to take NCII seriously. Despite legislation, few cases result in charges due to victim withdrawal, police inaction, or prosecutorial hesitation. Specialized training, clearer CPS guidelines, and trauma-informed practices are needed to ensure the justice system does not retraumatize victims.

Prioritize Education and Public Awareness
Rather than focusing solely on law and tech, the authors emphasize preventive education as a critical tool. This includes embedding digital consent, image-based abuse, and respectful relationships into curricula and public campaigns. Education helps shift the cultural norms that enable NCII, reduces stigma, and empowers potential victims with knowledge and resources.

Build a Global Victim Support Ecosystem
A global, culturally competent, and multilingual network of support services is essential. The book suggests expanding NGO networks, aligning with international standards, and ensuring support is accessible across borders and demographics. This global infrastructure must be sustained with long-term funding and consistent policy alignment.

In conclusion, this book underscores that addressing Non-Consensual Intimate Image (NCII) abuse effectively demands a structural overhaul of the digital safety ecosystem. It is no longer sufficient to rely on piecemeal legislation, reactive enforcement, ad hoc victim support or excessive reliance on platform liability. Instead, what is required is a paradigm shift-anchored in survivor agency, backed by enforceable international frameworks, powered by ethical technology, and sustained through education, funding, and global collaboration. The UK's experience, particularly through the Revenge Porn Helpline, offers a replicable blueprint for effective, rights-based intervention. But meaningful progress hinges on political will, cross-sector cooperation, and a collective commitment to building a safer, more dignified digital world for all.

Index

S. Mortimer et al., *Ten Years of the Revenge Porn Helpline*, Palgrave Studies in Victims and Victimology, https://doi.org/10.1007/978-3-032-00614-1

FSC
www.fsc.org
MIX
Papier | Fördert gute Waldnutzung
FSC® C083411

Kolibri 360 GmbH
Ferdinand-Jühlke-Straße 7
99095 Erfurt, Deutschland
produktsicherheit@kolibri360.de